Realities of Business: Misadventures and Lessons Learnt

.

Peter Spinda

.

Peter Spinda Publishing

Peter Spinda Publishing

Spinda, Peter

Realities of Business: Misadventures and Lessons Learnt

First Edition: January 2012

This Revised Second Edition: March 2015

Brisbane, QLD, Australia

ISBN: 978-0-9872627-6-9

To my wife Kitty.

Thank you for being so awesome.

To my daughter Sophia and my boys Alex and Mika.

Become Leaders. Not Followers.

Chapter Index

Realities of Business: Misadventures and Lessons Learnt

FOREWORD

The first rule of business: Embrace Failure

The world of business in my opinion is complex yet basic, exciting yet exhausting, often times presenting problems and challenges that question our own self beliefs and capabilities.

For those who have yet to experience running or managing a business, it would be difficult to appreciate just what it takes to launch into a new business venture or to successfully run a profitable organisation. The traditional rules of an employee do not apply to business owners, as the realities of business are often far harsher than the 'comfort' of being an employee.

A number of years ago at the age of 19, I decided to launch head first into a business venture. I knew nothing about business, nothing about management and very little about financial planning. What I had were dreams of business riches, of success at a young age. I would often dream of my life a few years down the track, where I would be the head of my own start up organization that had become a national success story. I would be driving an expensive sports car and people would recognise me as that young guy who made millions from his first business. Suffice to say, the realities of business were quite different to the ones I had imagined and created in my head.

Don't get me wrong, dreaming is important. We must have goals to strive towards, and dreams to keep us going during the tough times, but we must also ensure that we keep check of what is really possible and what is realistic. As I have experienced over the years, reality can be a very cruel and harsh teacher. But what I have also learnt is that with the right approach and the right attitude it really is possible to become successful in business.

Over the past 15 years (and counting) I have started multiple businesses from nothing, turning ideas into profitable ventures. I have experienced all of the highs and lows that business owners inevitably go through. At times I've been on top of the world, at the head of a successful business with several employees, the bank account had plenty of money in it and I had commitment from clients. Then there were moments of anger and frustration as business collapsed, which in the worst scenario caused me to spiral into depression and self loathing, an outcome that would take its toll on my personal life and relationships with loved ones.

Despite all the 'crap' that goes with running a business, I still wouldn't have it any other way. If you are determined, persistent and strong willed, business can give you a rush and excitement that compares with the adrenaline of extreme sports. It can give you control of your destiny and can set you up financially for life. The key is to be patient, to not rush and to plan your moves strategically and with intent.

I often think to myself 'if only I knew back when I was 19 what I know now, my life and ventures would have most likely turned out very differently'. But alas, one cannot turn back time. All you can do is reflect and learn from your failures; and make sure that next time around you don't go down the same path and make the same mistakes. Failing in business has made me acutely aware of my knowledge and capabilities, and has given me more valuable lessons than what a University degree in business ever would.

The harsh reality is that most businesses will fail within a few short years of starting up. As such, the first rule I have in business is to <u>Embrace Failure</u>. Should you decide to get into business, you will no doubt go through some tough times that will test your will and commitment, and eventually you will be faced with two choices:

1. Get frustrated about the situation, which will magnify your failure and cause you to experience significant stress and pressure, or ,

2. Embrace the situation, use it to fuel your drive to challenge and conquer the problems facing you and your business.

And you know what? Even if you can't conquer your problem and the business folds, you will have learnt valuable lessons that will help you succeed in your next venture.

In the words of the wise Buddha: *'let failure be a lesson, let suffering be your strength, let love overcome all your barriers'.*

Pete

SECTION 1

My story.

GET HEALTHY

My first business

When I was 19, a brief moment of impatience led to the beginning of my first business venture.

It was July 1999, the start of the second university semester. The time had come again to wait *patiently* in line outside the university book shop to purchase our next lot of overpriced (and in my case underutilized) textbooks. I was studying to become a chiropractor, with plans of going on to study medicine and eventually become an orthopedic surgeon. My book list was long, and I knew from talking to others that I was going to be broke after this purchase. Nonetheless, I needed these books, so I had no choice but wait in line like everyone else.

After standing for about half an hour in a line that wound its way amongst the campus buildings like a snake in a maze, my patience was coming to an end. I kept thinking to myself, 'this is such bullshit; not only do they take our money, but they also make us wait'. After a further 5 minutes I had enough and jumped out of the line, determined to find a better solution. I stormed off to the computer lab located inside the library and with a smug grin on my face I sat down in front of a computer. I was quite pleased with my *smart* idea - I'll just buy all my books online and have them shipped direct to my door. It was a simple enough idea, but to my amazement no matter what I searched, I could not find a website that sold and shipped all of the books I needed to Australia. An hour later I found myself at the end of the bookshop line again. This time I didn't care about the wait; my mind was off racing with ideas, as something inside me that had never surfaced before burst through and automatically took control of my thoughts. Before I realized, I was inside the bookshop and by this time I had come up with the idea to start my own business!

I consider this day to be a significant turning point in my life, a point that has changed the way I think about myself, my goals and the world around me. This day was the start of a passion that had been waiting inside me to be uncovered. My life prior to this day had always revolved around studying to become a doctor, which meant that my focus and my world was driven by the requirements and experiences necessary to make this a reality. As a result, I had limited exposure to the world of business and in truth knew nothing about setting up and running a business. What I did know was that to become a doctor I would have to devote a lot of time to study, which meant spending my remaining free time working so I can support myself through Uni. This also meant not having a life outside work and study. Like other financially struggling university students I was keen to make an extra buck, so the idea of making money *easily* through a business was very appealing. At this stage the world of business looked simple enough, and it was with this naivety and easy money expectation that my entrepreneurial journey began.

I spent the following few months researching publishers and reading up on starting a business. I immersed myself in a myriad of business and finance books, often times reading them in my lectures instead of paying attention to the course content. Of course, none of the books I read told me or warned me of the dangers ahead. All talked about the riches, the wealth and the success, forgetting to mention the fact that the vast majority of businesses fail in the first few years, with a very low percentage surviving and being successful past the 5 year mark. Nor did they go into detail about the personal dedication and struggles that almost all business owners face at some stage; struggles that can lead to the breakdown of relationships and medical problems such as depression and anxiety.

The Start

Like a cocky teenager who believes they know the road after just passing their drivers license examination, I was convinced I knew everything about business after reading a few books. Armed with my *supposed* complete knowledge, in December 1999 I proceeded to hit my business idea at full speed (in between full time studies, relationship and part time work).

I spent much of my summer holiday that year laying the foundations of the business, focusing initially on securing all of the suppliers. I didn't yet have a business registered, but I did have an idea for a name: Get Healthy. This name signified the core ideology that I had as a healthcare student – that to live a happy life we had to get healthy and stay healthy. By around March 2000 I had succeeded in convincing the relevant publishers to sell to me in bulk and at a discount. I must add however that pulling this off was trickier than I had planned.

Actually, come to think of it, I had no real plan of action; I seriously thought that suppliers would welcome my phone call with open arms, ready to give me a massive discount so I can sell their books through my business. I was therefore surprised and taken back when my calls resulted in a bombardment of questions for which I was unprepared. In addition, I was told that if I wanted to do business I had to go and meet them in person, put forth a business case and apply for a purchasing account with them. Put simply, no one was prepared to give me an account over the phone.

Left with no choice, I lined up back to back meetings with the suppliers. I borrowed a suit from a friend, bought a new tie and prepared a set of answers based on the questions they asked me over the phone. Having never been in a business meeting before, I was ultra nervous when the day came. My mouth was dry and my palms were covered in a sheen of sweat that refused to go away.

My performance in the meetings was poor at best; my voice shook, sweat beads formed on my forehead and my answers sounded as though I had just learnt the use of grammar. It didn't help my cause that at the age of 19 I looked more like a 16 year old teenager who had just gone through his pimply puberty stage!

All of the meetings went the same way: the account managers told me of their company, their rules and requirements around setting up accounts, and their expectations from distributors in a manner that can be likened to a parent telling their child the conditions of going over to a friend's house for a sleep over. After setting a sobering scene, the metaphorical microphone got handed over to me to explain what a pubescent looking 19 year old with sweaty palms and shaky nervous voice was doing in their meeting room. Needless to say I was taken aback by the process and expectations. Again my naivety shone through as I thought that I would walk into these meetings and have them bow over me, shake my hand in excitement as if I had just delivered them a winning lottery ticket, all because I wanted to sell their products and represent their company in the market place. In reality, faced with what looked like a time wasting teenager, rather than be over the moon at being able to sell more products, publishers were more concerned about my ability to pay an account and even manage my business!

Perhaps they felt sorry for me, or maybe they really did see potential in the idea, but after I was given the chance to explain my book shop dilemma and the idea to solve this in my own bumbling and nervous way, I managed to secure not just one, but all of the suppliers. Overall the terms were not very favorable, with discounts that only gave me a small margin of a few percent per item. I didn't care about this though, I was confident that once orders started rolling in and the publishers saw the business take off I could negotiate better deals. I even managed to dance around the fact that the business at that stage was not yet in existence, using the *cheeky* line that registration was in progress. In reality, I was holding off as I had virtually no money and wanted to ensure I could line up all the suppliers prior to spending the money required to register the business.

In Australia, setting up a simple sole trading business comprises of 2 components:

1. Register a business name.

2. Register the actual business with the Government and acquire an Australian Business Number (ABN).

Shortly after securing the supplier agreements I registered the business name of Get Healthy, in preparation for officially starting the business later that year. Around this time, one of my friends, John (not his real name), approached me about wanting to be a part of my grand idea. After giving it a good 5 minute thought I agreed to take him on as an equal partner, figuring that two heads were better than one! Due to the costs involved in setting up a company we agreed to register the business initially under my name as a sole trader, and so, my first business was registered on the 30 July 2000, using my previously registered trading name of Get Healthy.

In the lead up to the business registration, John and I launched our first ever marketing campaign. Knowing that the second semester of University was to start in July and students started purchasing their books from May onwards, we spent May – July promoting our yet to be registered and opened business. We created a bunch of simple fliers and posted them all over the University campus. We also took advantage of the projectors and chairs located in lecture rooms by sneaking in just before lectures, placing fliers on all chairs, as well as projecting the flier on the massive lecture boards. Lecturers hassled us initially for this, but as we just keep doing it, eventually they gave up and some even gave us a few minutes at the beginning of the lecture to talk to the students as a group!

The first orders were taken verbally as students approached us, with this evolving within a few weeks to an order form we had printed on the back of the fliers. All payments were to be made in cash, upfront and at time of ordering. Once we had a bunch of sales we placed our first orders with our suppliers, and as a sign of good faith used the cash paid upfront from the students to pay for our orders upfront as well, rather than using the 7 or 14 day account terms.

To keep costs low for our customers we avoided posting orders direct, and opted to personally deliver the completed orders. John and I would sort and compile each order, then pack them into the boot of his car to be delivered at allocated pick up times from the University parking lot.

I should point out at this stage that although the initial idea was to setup an online shop selling textbooks, I decided to hold off on this until I had tested the idea in the marketplace. I really wanted an online presence, but I also wanted to get selling fast without being bogged down with web design and setting up of merchant accounts. This is why I just got on with paper orders, and only months later did the online store finally come to fruition.

And so, business continued in this manner for the next 6 months - taking orders initially on pieces of paper then via email, and delivering the stock in the boot of John's car.

The Growth

As the months went by our product line started expanding, and we ventured away from purely book supplies. After realizing that the other big expense for students in our course was medical equipment, we decided to expand into this area and replicate what we were doing with books, securing accounts with a number of key medical and healthcare product manufacturers. This turned out to be a great decision on our part. As it happened, one of the main suppliers was planning a strong move into the student sector and we came along at the right time. They offered us a fantastic wholesale rate and payment terms that to this day I have never been able to replicate.

With orders steadily growing it was becoming harder for us to run things with our current setup. We would run around in between lectures either taking orders or running to the car to deliver orders. We had to expand our delivery schedule from twice a week to once a day. As a result of our poor system for taking and monitoring orders, we started making mistakes and a number of mix ups occurred. It was obvious that the idea had merit, but the current process was simply inadequate and inefficient.

To fix this problem, after much deliberation we decided it was time to get serious and move the business online, finally achieving my original dream of setting up an online textbook shop. We registered www.gethealthy.com.au, and with no money to spend on web design John and I tackled the creation of our website. Building on an initial template we found an out of the box website creation solution for $99. And so, with no web design experience ourselves, after many sleepless nights, our website was born.

Once all the products were uploaded into the back end database we linked it all with an online transaction gateway to our bank. This system finally enabled us to accept non cash payments using credit cards and ATM cards, and made our lives easier with the simple order placement and transaction processing; though it also came at a cost which ate into our meager profit margins. It was cheap to set up and host the site; what proved expensive were the various fees involved with maintaining the shopping trolley aspect of it. There were monthly account keeping fees with our bank and the transaction gateway provider. Then there was a percentage taken off by the payment gateway company from all transactions that were via credit cards, which accounted for almost 100% of our sales. These of course we didn't really consider or factor into our pricing, the effect of which you will read later on.

Prior to the launch of the site we were really restricted with our market. Not long after launching the site we received our first order from outside our University and state, making us a national business overnight. Surprisingly the order was placed by a medical student, a market that until then we hadn't even looked at as we were still just focusing on the chiropractic sector. Suffice to say my ideas starting flowing as I sat with John discussing this order. We were talking in uncontainable excitement about hitting the medical student market, a sector we knew would be worth a lot of dollars. Our luck with new opportunities didn't end there though. Whilst we were researching how to enter this market, another opportunity randomly presented itself.

One afternoon I had just placed a fresh lot of posters around the University campus advertising our services (after they had been taken down for the millionth time), when I was approached by an economics student. He had seen our posters and was asking whether we could source him his course books for the year. Of course, true to my nature, without hesitation I said sure, we can definitely help! I took his details and found myself an hour later scrambling around sourcing accounts with various economics textbook publishers. This, combined with our one order from a medical student, led to the grand idea – let's forget about just our course and let's supply all books for every tertiary course existent in Australia! We were confident in the idea (we did no research to back up our confidence, it just 'felt' right). However, we were very short on money to bring such an idea to reality. Rather than wait until we secured our current market and our sales increased to a point where we had the cash (profit) available in our bank account, we impatiently decided to speed things up and sourced funds from an external investor. I had a family friend that showed a lot of interest in the idea and in June 2001 I signed my first investment agreement. In hindsight, I should have had the process managed by a solicitor. The agreement that was written up left a lot of 'what if's' unanswered, contained a lot of ambiguity and didn't cover off on some very important points that would later come back to cause issues.

We ended our first year in business and our first financial year (FY) on a high - full of excitement about our new ideas and the possibilities that lay ahead. Inadvertently though, without knowing, this decision to diversify too much, too quickly, would lead to the demise of my first company.

Year 2 of running Get Healthy was absolutely crazy. I spent most of my time either struggling to sit through lectures and studying for exams, or working in the business, dreaming of grand success and huge riches. I was devouring all sorts of business related books, with my declining grades at University being a testament to my lack of interest and care for what I was studying.

July 2001, the start of Year 2 in business, saw us take the next step with the business structure and transitioned from a sole trading business to that of a company. We registered Get Healthy Australia Proprietary Limited, my first company, with a 50/50 equal shareholding between John and I. I have to say I was feeling pretty good about myself as the New Year started off, and my cockiness was at an all time high. I made new business cards, giving myself the very important sounding title of 'Director', and sped forward at full speed taking on the new ideas without giving them the logical analysis or thinking they deserved, and needed!

The first issue we tackled was the website. The initial out of the box solution was quickly becoming outdated and unusable given the amount of products we were adding into the system. After spending many all nighters learning html coding and playing with graphics software, version 2 of the gethealthy.com.au site went live. The feedback from customers was positive and we were now receiving orders every day of the week from chiropractic and medical students around Australia.

With the rapid growth of the business came a whole new set of challenges and problems. Having never dealt with financials before, I took a crash course in business accounting by reading a few web articles and attending a Department of Taxation lecture on basic business taxation. Whilst this information helped me realize that there is more to business financials than just looking at the bank balance every now and then, I failed to properly utilize the new information. Profit and loss statements, budgets, expense sheets etc were all still foreign, and as I still had my cocky attitude that everything will work out perfectly we didn't think they were necessary. Whenever it crossed my mind, I would check our bank balance and look at outstanding invoices. As a result, I had no visibility as to how much money we were actually making or how much it really cost to run the business.

Logistics was another headache.

Shipments were leaving our makeshift warehouse (aka John's parents garage) every day, but with our focus being all over the place it was only a matter of time before we stuffed something up. Only a few months into the 2nd year we experienced our first hiccups around incorrect shipments, products being returned and refunds or discounts having to be issued. We quickly realized that if we didn't pull our heads in and focus, it could all come tumbling down around us.

To avoid this, we came up with a daily routine that worked very well for us based on the current volumes, maximizing our time efficiency. John handled the majority of the accounts side of things, I dealt mainly with marketing and we both sold and packaged products. A production line was setup to ensure all orders leaving our hands were 100% accurate, thanks to a double checking system we developed. In the background, we were also actively working on setting up accounts in a myriad of other disciplines and creating a massive database of textbooks in preparation for our grand venture.

The biggest challenge of this 2nd year, however, was not the website, financials or logistics, but the one thing that we could not easily control: time. Our University course was becoming demanding, whilst at the same time business was coming in the door daily and took up just as much of our time. It was certainly a challenging period for us both personally, especially given the fact that for all this hard work we still weren't receiving any significant financial benefits. Everything we earned was being pumped back into the business, in the hope that we would strike gold soon enough!

We expanded our marketing strategies this year and partnered up with a number of student organizations in an attempt to corner the market. In return for their support, i.e. promoting us to all of their members, we agreed to sponsor various student events throughout the year. We achieved the desired results from these partnerships, solidifying us in the marketplace and giving us the confidence boost we needed to keep pushing forward.

Despite all the turmoil and mistakes, we actually made a little profit by the end of Year 2. However, because profits were redirected back into the company, neither of us drew an income and we were still working for free! In hindsight we should have continued along this path, further solidifying the business in our niche chiropractic and medical markets before taking the huge leap forward that the coming year would bring.

By the start of our 3rd year in business, July 2002, we had opened accounts with well over 200 publishers and various suppliers, and had over 10,000 products in our database. We were still only selling via the gethealthy.com.au website and only selling chiropractic and medical textbooks and products, but in the background the plan to launch the new site, catering for our now expanded client and product base, was taking shape. In preparation we were developing a new website, updating our database of products and working through a marketing strategy. The planned launch date: January 2003.

This 3rd year in business started very successfully, and overall revenue for the year increased by over 500% on our prior year's revenue! We had turned over several hundred thousand dollars in revenue; however, as you will read, such quick growth caught us off guard and resulted in a whole lot of problems.

This year was also of significant personal importance. After much deliberation I decided to discontinue my studies, and in December 2002 I officially pulled out of the Masters Degree I was undertaking. My parents were horrified. Despite my efforts to explain, no one understood why I would pull out after studying for 5 years with only one more year to go. It was a very tough decision, but I knew I had done the right thing and I was able to focus solely on Get Healthy.

With the database revamp nearing completion it was time to look at moving forward with our next project – the new and improved website. The first thing we had to do was register a new business name and obtain a new domain, as Get Healthy was too specific for our needs. We wanted something easy to spell, a name that would not restrict us with where we could take the business. After looking at dozens of possibilities and searching hundreds of domain availabilities, we stumbled across the word 'Goby'. It was what we were after – an easy to spell word that was available as a domain. It didn't actually have any meaning to us (although goby is a type of fish!), it just sounded cool and easy to remember! Without hesitation we registered this as our new trading name under the existing company name.

Before I continue with this story, I would like to take a side step and tell you about another misadventure that played out simultaneously...

The Syringe Side Step

I was very much all over the place in my early 20s and possessed the attention span of a flea. As you would have gathered by now, I was also very spontaneous and would jump from idea to idea, not giving anything much thought or consideration. It was this personality trait that caused me to take a side step whilst working on my Goby venture and pursue a product that was completely off track from that venture.

One morning whilst flicking through a newspaper an article caught my eye. It was a story on a local inventor who succeeded in raising funds for a new invention – the retractable syringe. What made the product unique was that unlike a normal syringe, this one had a needle which retracted into the plastic body after use. I could see that this was a great invention, one that could help prevent people from being stuck by potentially virus-infected disposed needles in parks and beaches, and could prevent medical staff from potentially serious needle stick injuries whilst on the job. Excitedly, seeing venture possibilities, I found myself on the web searching the world for similar products. My idea: I would find a similar product already in existence and would beat the local inventor to the market. His product was still in the research and development stage, so I knew I had at least two years up my sleeve before he would start full scale production.

It didn't take long before I stumbled across what I was looking for. It was a product already being sold and used across the UK and US, and from what I saw they had no distributors for the Australian/New Zealand regions. It had a similar concept, although the design and mechanism was totally different to the one invented locally. I proceeded to get in touch with the manufacturer, and after several weeks of extensive communications via email and a couple of phone calls we came to an agreement - John and I would seriously look at this product range and its viability in the Australian market.

It was at this stage that again my naivety and lack of business experience shone through, and if I were to do things again, I can tell you the approach would be completely different. But I guess one has to learn the hard way sometimes...

Obtaining several thousand dollars from my parents, John and I went ahead with ordering several hundred samples and brochures, at our cost, from the manufacturer. Upon receipt of the above mentioned goods, John and I hit the ground running at full speed ahead. First of all we got on the phone and emails and started talking to various clinics, hospitals and government agencies around Australia to work out who would be interested in buying such products. It took a few months but after a bit of persistence we managed to get a number of interested parties who wanted us to come and demonstrate the products to them. Whilst this was going on, we were keeping up the regular communication with the manufacturer. We were also busy with the main Goby business and this was certainly a time of major juggling - textbooks, to syringes and back to textbooks! I often asked myself why I created so many headaches for myself – but I just kept ignoring any doubts with complete stubbornness.

With contacts established, John and I decided to get on the road and start demonstrating our new syringe range. As we had both been to a number of business meetings by this stage of our business careers, we were quietly confident that we could pull off sales without too many issues. Of course the meetings didn't quite go as planned. First of all, we were totally underprepared for the line of questions we were hit with. In addition, we didn't make any sales. In fact, we found out that in order to make sales to these organizations we had to jump through several hoops, including completing tender documentation and submitting detailed research data. It wasn't going to be the quick sale we were after. It was going to be a laborious time and resource consuming task that would take many months before any decisions on purchases will be made and announced.

We were determined to succeed at this though and didn't let these potential obstacles put a damper on our efforts. Discussions with our manufacturer around an exclusive distribution contract for the Australian market continued, and after a lot of back and forth we got an email advising us that the company Vice President was going to come to Australia to meet John and I to sign off on the distribution agreement. We were very excited about this news and arranged everything from hotel accommodation to car rental and a number of client meetings for this important person (our VIP) to attend with us. So excited were we that true to form we weren't looking at the whole picture and totally missed one really important step: getting a copy of the agreement well in advance of the meeting and reviewing it with legal advice. Never been burnt before,

I had faith that the agreement would be favourable for us both and that we would easily sign off on everything.

After weeks of anxious waiting, the day finally arrived for the Vice President's visit. Waiting for her at the Sydney International Airport John and I held up a sign with her name on it. Through the crowd an attractive woman in her late 40's started walking towards us, looking left and right, in search of a familiar face, before looking right through the crowd and seeing her name on our sign. If only I had a video camera to record her face the moment she realized that we were the Australian business men she had come to meet. Here we were, two young guys in our very early 20's, seeking to sign a multimillion dollar contract with a very successful international company. I knew the instant she laid eyes on me that we were going to have issues. The car ride to her hotel was uneventful. Not much conversation took place; it was obvious she was not impressed with us. As we dropped her off at the hotel she gave us a copy of the contract to read through and sign off on. That evening we took her out to an expensive fancy restaurant (which we paid for), after which we agreed to pick her up at 9am the next morning to start off our client visits.

I wore my nicest shirt and tie the next day, and John and I were still quite excited about the whole deal the next morning as we walked into the lobby of her hotel. The excitement however didn't last long. We walked to reception and asked for them to buzz up to our VIP's room so that she knows we are waiting downstairs. You can imagine my shock when reception said to us 'I'm sorry, but Mrs. VIP has already checked out'. Of course we thought she made a mistake, so we asked her to check the system. It wasn't our day however. She shook her head as she looked at the computer screen, and we immediately knew that our VIP had run away on us! It was an unbelievable scenario, but given her facial expression when she realized who we were at the airport and her unimpressed attitude that whole day, we should have guessed that something was up.

John and I sat down in the lobby of the hotel and for a good ten minutes we both just starred at the floor, not uttering a single word. We ended up sitting there for over an hour, quietly talking through the myriad of 'what next' questions that came out of this situation.

Later that day back at John's place, we finally decided to look through the contract. It was an incredibly comprehensive document that took quite some time to read through. It was then that it occurred to me that even if this VIP was interested in working with us, signing the contract would have been impossible given what they were after. There were minimum order amounts to meet per month, there were marketing requirements and there was even the requirement for regular trips to the US to liaise closely with the manufacturers. To put this in context, they were expecting orders worth multiple million dollars every quarter – a phenomenal amount that to us seemed so out of reach that we were astonished the whole deal got so far down the track without either party ever discussing this!

Despite knowing that there was no point pursuing the matter via the legal system, I was so furious with the situation that we decided to try anyway. Of course all this achieved was wasting a couple more thousand dollars of our money, all to no effect. There was nothing that could be done about the situation except to reflect and learn. An expensive mistake indeed, and so poorly executed that I am to this day embarrassed about how the deal went down.

Back to Goby...

So back to our new website for Goby. This site had to be robust enough to handle large volumes of traffic, had to be very user friendly and had to look professional. Had we the money to invest into this I would have outsourced such development instantly, but alas this was not the case. John and I knuckled down, got behind our computers yet again and spent weeks working ridiculous hours to finally have a site that met our needs and ticked all the right boxes.

Whilst developing the new site, John and I would have excited conversations about where we saw the business going. Ideas flowed freely and using a large whiteboard that I had hanging in the computer room I would draw mind maps and plans with bright colored markers. The future that I saw for Goby grew much broader than the textbooks we had started out on, and was aimed at fulfilling the needs of students.

These are the areas I had in mind:

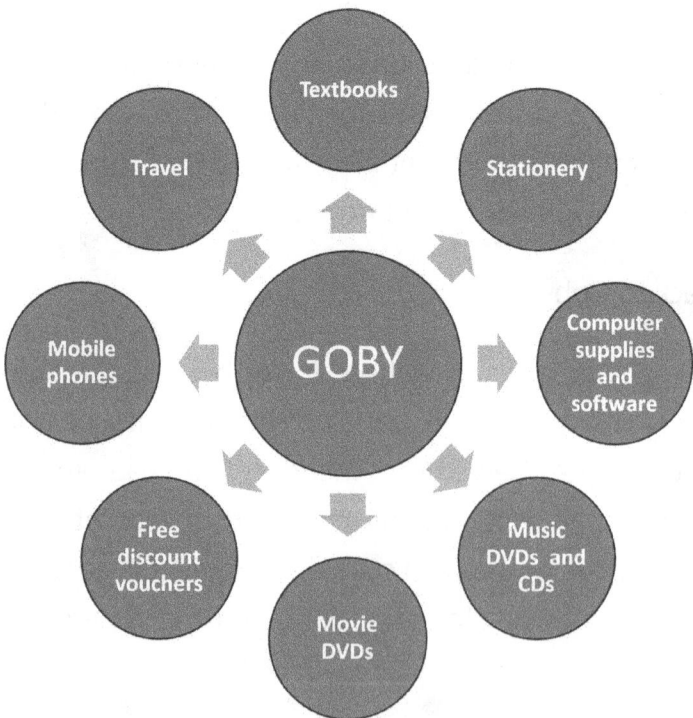

It was a grand idea and I had every intention of achieving this goal. Unfortunately, as with many of my ideas, the execution proved much more complex and demanding than I had first thought. The first non-educational products we tried to expand into were CDs, DVDs and mobile phone plans. To initially keep things 'simple', we partnered up with a large international music store chain for the CD/DVD distribution. They would give me the weekly top 20 charts that would go on our site, and all orders for CDs/DVDs would go directly through to their logistics. In return we would get a percentage cut from the deal. I also struck a deal with a telecommunications company who was keen to use Goby as part of a campaign for their new range of mobile products. The deal was similar to the CDs/DVDs, and again seemed quite simple. We designed the new site with both of these categories available, making sure that the agreements were in place by the time the site was made live.

Marketing

In anticipation of a January 2003 rollout of the website, we developed a multiple pronged marketing strategy. This consisted of:

1. The creation of large timetable posters.
2. An on-campus promotions team (Goby reps).

3. Free media publicity.
4. Hosting on-campus student BBQs.

The Plan

The purpose of the timetables was to give students something they could have hanging on their walls, something they could use and refer to regularly throughout the year. To make it more effective I designed the poster to be big, about the size of a movie poster you see hanging in cinemas. We were to print 10,000 copies (not sure where this number came from), and planned to distribute them to every university campus dorm in the country. We were also to send out a poster with every order and my reps were to hand them out at university campuses. To help cover the cost of printing and distribution I planned to sell advertising space at a rate of $9,000 per ad, with 6 available spaces. To minimize expenses, I also decided to design the whole poster myself, with no external help.

Whilst the posters were printing, we were to employ (on a commission only basis) a team of reps in the larger universities around Australia to represent Goby on campus throughout the university year. They were to market Goby, take orders and answer any product/order related questions. With the help of the reps, we were to organize free student BBQs at several universities at the start of the year. I also wanted to obtain free publicity in local and national newspapers, in the form of a cover story on the business. The overall goal of the multi-pronged approach was to increase our brand awareness nationally and generate us a heap of revenue.

Even though the campaign was ultimately successful, how it transpired to this day amuses me, and after reading this section I am sure you will shake your head and ask yourself 'why!?'

The Execution

The execution of the strategy was haphazard and time consuming, but surprisingly successful!

The design and printing of the posters went without a hitch. 10,000 beautiful quality full color posters were delivered to us after only a few weeks, although they did give us an unexpected headache as we didn't realize just how much storage space so many posters needed. Now, remember how I had planned to sell 6 advertising spots? Well, I actually managed to pull it off... Sort of...

I contacted a variety of large businesses to promote their services/products on our posters, ranging from burger sellers to coffee sellers to book publishers. Most said no, but a condom manufacturer, a clothing company, café franchise, energy drinks producer and a medical devices manufacturer took a chance and said yes! There was only one catch with all of them - none wanted to pay money. They did however all offer alternatives – products or discounts in exchange for the advertisement. I guess you can see where this is going...... In hindsight we really should have negotiated this better, but at the time it seemed like a good idea to negotiate no further and accept this suggestion. And so it was to John's parents' horror, that shortly after they had to deal with 10,000 posters delivered to their house, over a 24 hour period we had managed to completely use up all their garage space with 9,000 cans of energy drinks and 10,000 individually packaged strawberry flavored condoms!!

Yes, I will say it again, at the time it actually seemed like a brilliant idea. Luckily the coffee shop just sent us various discount vouchers via email to distribute to customers, the medical manufacturer gave us some free products and an extra discount off our wholesale pricing, while the clothing shop agreed to dress all my reps for free and gave John and I free clothes.

While the above 'awesome' negotiating took place, we began the recruitment process to hire the university campus reps. It didn't take long before we had secured 9 reps and a few friends on the ground for the first few weeks of the university semester. My quest to obtain free publicity also went well as I managed to score an article written on the business in The Australian newspaper, which also featured a full colored photo of John and I! Overall, we had achieved everything planned in the multi-pronged strategy and was thrilled about it.

Taking a few steps back now, before we were ready however to launch the marketing campaign and our new site, we had to tackle our biggest headache: logistics.

Logistics

As the business was growing at a rapid pace, more and more of our time had to be spent on packaging and shipping. We were quickly running to run out of warehousing and working space at Johns parents place (the garage was already full), which was a big concern as we were anticipating Goby to be much bigger than Get Healthy ever was. In my usual way I was expecting big things from the business and so decided that we needed a more professional approach to the whole issue of logistics. It didn't take long before we identified a list of businesses that could help with our dilemma, and in a space of about a week John and I met with a number of representatives from some of Australia's largest logistics companies. After much discussion and going back and forth, we eventually came to an agreement with one company to outsource all of our warehousing and logistics using their just launched electronic system.

The agreement and setup came at a hefty price upfront, but at the time we were confident of the return it would generate. Apart from the upfront costs, there would also be ongoing running costs that included a small fee we had to pay per item for every day it sat on their warehousing shelves. This seemed negligible at the time, so we proceeded forward. With the agreement signed, the process of marrying up our systems and databases with theirs began. The overall plan was to eliminate us ever having to see any of the products or even have to order them in from manufacturers/publishers.

Have a look at the diagram on the following page, comparing our existing logistics set up with the new one.

Existing:

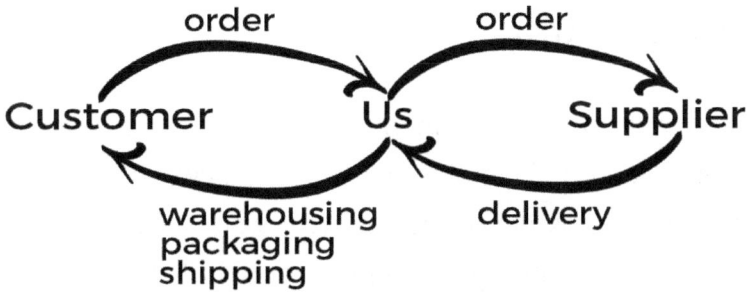

New:

As you can see, outsourcing the whole logistics process made good sense. Not only did it free up our resources, but it also cut down on shipping costs for customers while providing free tracking and faster turnaround times. As a result of the agreement, we now had warehousing and shipping points in the three east coast Australian cities of Brisbane, Sydney and Melbourne.

We had a dedicated team allocated to our business and I have to say I felt like a mini king running my own successful company!

Marketing Success

With everything now in place the marketing strategy was kicked off. Several thousand posters were mailed to campus dorms nationally. The rest were handed out in Goby show bags by my reps throughout the first few weeks of the start of the New Year, which also included one condom, one energy drink and various other vouchers and Goby promo flyers. We had also planned to send a show bag with each order, but had to skip sending cans of drinks and the large posters due to the postal logistics and cost involved. In the end the reps didn't work out too well. Being on commission only, they realized that it was not the easy money generator they had hoped for and all gave up a few weeks in.

All in all though, the article featuring us in The Australian did wonders for the business, and we considered the campaign a success (although when the business was eventually wound down I was stuck with thousands of energy drinks and condoms!! A likely combination!).

Like a shot of adrenalin into the system, the marketing campaign launched the business forward at a pace we could only have dreamed of.

I was on top of the world, business was taking off at a pace that far outweighed my expectations and we were finally making money. Unfortunately it was at this point, where the business started growing so rapidly, that cracks began to form.

With the marketing plan in full swing the orders flooded in, taking us by surprise. So much so that in the 3 months following Goby's launch we generated about 3 x as much revenue as we did the whole prior financial year!

With the orders coming in thick and fast, it was no surprise that we quickly ran into two major problems, one following the other:

1. Running out of stock.

2. System flaws for logistics.

Beginning of the End

Stock Issues

The first problem was running out of stock and underestimating the volume of orders. To deal with this, we initially had to advise our customers of a delay in shipping and offer a full refund of their money if they did not want to wait. Luckily the delay was only a week or so, and the majority held on. However, just as we got on top of the orders, the problem got worse. Our publishers advised us that they had run out of stock on all of the popular titles that we were selling – waiting time growing to 2 weeks. We advised customers and continued selling the titles. 2 weeks however became 3, which turned into 4 and so on. Receiving complaint after complaint, we ended up refunding more orders than were coming in.

Logistics Issues

The second problem came from the logistics side of things. The system we had relied on had a number of flaws, none of which became apparent until integration was complete and the orders were flowing heavily. As we ran out of stock many partial orders started piling up on the shelves, waiting to be completed. As the backlog stock started coming in from suppliers, one would think that older orders got filled first then the newer ones. But for some reason it was happening the other way, and so some orders that could have been filled with little delay ended up sitting on the shelf longer and longer. And of course this just made things worse for 2 reasons:

1. Students talked amongst themselves, word of mouth spread, and many customers complained about not receiving goods, but their friends, who ordered the same books weeks after them, had already received them.

2. Valuable stock that could have gone out to customers was sitting on the shelves, costing us money in warehousing fees for each day it sat there.

The problems reached a peak when somehow (we would never receive an explanation for this) a multitude of orders got mixed up by the logistics company and, you guessed it, we had to face a bunch of irate, angry customers. We ended up seeking compensation from the logistics company over this stuff up, as the value of incorrect orders was in the order of many thousands of dollars. As a result of the issues, only 4 months after launching Goby we cancelled our contract with the logistics company and brought logistics in-house once again.

On top of all the stock and logistical issues we were facing, the DVD, CD and mobile phone plan idea proved to be a huge headache and more of a hassle than it was worth. It was difficult to keep the data feed from suppliers accurate and up to date with all the chaos around us. In addition to that, orders containing both books and CDs were especially difficult to process as the CDs were being shipped straight to the customer, bypassing our logistics company. Keeping track of these orders and reconciling them proved time consuming and not worth the meager profits we made on them. In the end we canned this idea just weeks into the launch of the new site.

There was however an even bigger problem brewing: serious damage had been done to our reputation as a result of the logistics bungle.

Downward Spiral

What went up so quickly came tumbling down just as quick. Sales plummeted just months after experiencing dizzying heights and we had gone from strong profits to a serious question mark over the future viability of the business.

Having to refund so many orders cost us a lot of money; just have a look at the bottom diagram to see where we were bleeding so much money:

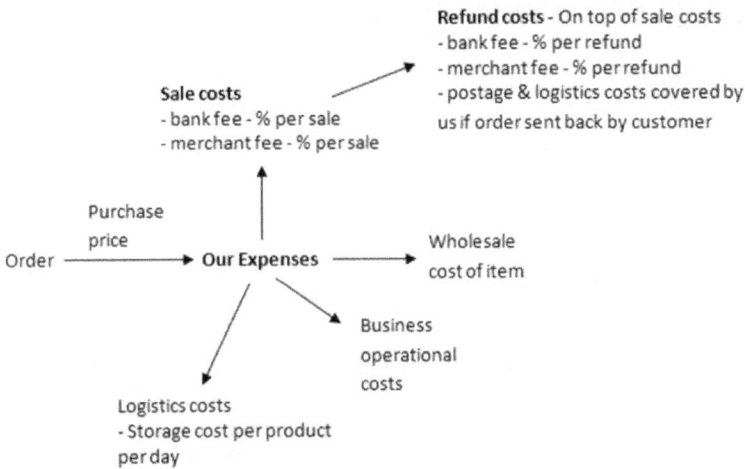

Refund costs - On top of sale costs
- bank fee - % per refund
- merchant fee - % per refund
- postage & logistics costs covered by us if order sent back by customer

Sale costs
- bank fee - % per sale
- merchant fee - % per sale

Purchase price

Order ———→ **Our Expenses** ———→ Wholesale cost of item

Business operational costs

Logistics costs
- Storage cost per product per day

To sum up, as orders were paid online we lost a certain percentage from each sale to our bank and merchant provider in the form of transaction fees. When orders were refunded, again we lost money as we had to pay the same bank and merchant fees as that of a sales transaction. On top of this, we also had to pay the warehousing fees per item per day. As orders were not going out and instead sat on shelves, this was becoming an expensive exercise. These costs ate into our meager profit margins, and the overall result put us into an unfortunate predicament. Six months after the new launch our sales slowed to a dribble, we went full circle with our logistics, we were housing a heap of stock that we didn't know if we could sell and we had large bills from our suppliers that we didn't know how we would deal with. I was stunned at just how quickly we had gone from several hundred thousand dollars worth of sales in the first 3 months, to our nasty predicament not long after!

From what I saw there were two options:

1. Return all stock and shut the business facing some loss.

2. Keep going and risk either a bigger loss or even potential bankruptcy.

After so much time and energy invested I refused to give in. To me, there was only one answer – keep going and not give up. At this point John decided to leave the business and pursue his own studies and other interests. I was saddened by this as he was an excellent business partner, but knew he had to follow his passions.

I continued working on Goby; however, I was now in the following situation:

1. No business partner.

2. Bad credit with suppliers which forced me to pay at the time of order.

3. Business reputation tarnished.

4. Marketing could not continue due to being under resourced.

Borrowing further money from my parents and using my own credit card, I decided to be smarter with my inventory and logistics. First I transferred the operation of the business from Sydney to Brisbane – my parents' garage. I then assessed the biggest selling products to date and made a bulk order a few weeks before the start of the 2nd semester of University.

Once again though, inexperience and naivety got the better of me.

What I didn't realize was the actual impact marketing made in the 1st semester during the launch of Goby and just how tarnished our reputation became by the end of that semester only 6 months later! I did get orders, but they were small and few. I used the profit from those sales to pay off some of the very overdue accounts (some by many months!) but still, by the end of the year I was in more debt than I could deal with.

Throughout this stressful period there also occurred a shift in my thinking, energy and dedication toward the business, all of which sunk lower and lower. The debt was now sitting around $80,000 and I saw no way out.

Try as I might, I struggled to get back the momentum previously experienced. Sales dropped. I was stuck in a downward spiraling pit both with business and my personal psychological wellbeing. As business got worse, I lost more and more interest and struggled to find the physical and mental energy that I needed to keep going. It was a vicious circle.

The End

One miserable afternoon I started researching bankruptcy options and after a couple of weeks of deliberation made a call to an insolvency solicitor.

Given the situation, the news was better than I had expected. I could voluntarily liquidate the company and negotiate a deal with all of the creditors. I was happy to hear I could escape bankruptcy and not tarnish my credit record. The one thing that now stood in my way was the cost of undergoing liquidation. Having already borrowed plenty of money from my parents over the years, I didn't want to drag them further into this mess. So I went from bank to bank until one institution finally agreed to lend me the money I needed – albeit at a high interest rate, but better than nothing. Finally with my legal costs covered, a liquidator was appointed. They took control of the company, contacted all the creditors and negotiated outcomes with them. About 2 months later my company was officially wound down, closing after almost 5 years in business.

The Aftermath

Afterwards I felt battered, beat and incredibly down. I kept thinking of all the hard work, the many countless hours, weekends and nights I had spent working on my 'baby'. How could I have let myself fail so miserably? How could I have thought that I was skilled enough to run a business? These and many other thoughts haunted me. Depression is a horrid trap for the mind. It locks you in a well of deepening misery with low self esteem and low self worth. It took quite some time for me to get out of the mental darkness and it took a lot of strength to hide it from my family and friends. At the time it was impossible for me to appreciate the invaluable lesson this experience gave me. I feel I underwent a real life business course, a 'real world MBA'.

After a very short stint in real estate sales I landed a high paying sales rep job in the healthcare sector. The role was exciting and challenging, and as luck would have it the company was privately owned by a very successful entrepreneur who I knew I could learn a lot from.

OTHER IDEAS

About a year into this job I was approached by a competitor to work for them. They dangled a big carrot, made a lot of promises and I foolishly took the line. I left a position and company that I was perfectly suited for and joined a massive multinational, multibillion dollar corporate behemoth. Of course, the grass was not greener on the other side; in fact the environment was absolutely stifling for my entrepreneurial ways. I was missing the stimulation of really getting involved in a business and my mind kept wandering to thoughts of being my own boss again, running my own company again. I had many ideas, even tried a few including:

- Importing eyeglass frames and wholesaling to optical stores: This idea proved boring and as plenty of others were doing it, I didn't see a future in it.
- I then started my own men's clothing label "Pietro Gregori", selling ties and cufflinks after struggling to find good quality real silk ties at reasonable prices. I actually went to quite a bit of effort on this one and got a Chinese manufacturer to produce 10 different styles for me. I started by selling on eBay at first, and then sold them at the city markets and had an e-commerce website professionally developed by

a friend. I also got them into a number of retail stores around Brisbane. All up I invested about $10,000 into this business and ended up more than doubling my money. I decided however to not continue with this business for many reasons, the main one being my lack of passion or enthusiasm for the venture.

Ideas came and went, but the inner drive to run my own successful business just grew stronger and stronger. Fueled by a desire to break free from the traditional mould of society, I was scouting for business ideas wherever I went.

SPINDACORP

While working at the stifling multinational company, I did have one idea up my sleeve that I was quietly researching in the background. I knew it was viable, I just didn't quite know how to execute it. My job at the time required me to be present in operating theatres, throughout complex surgical procedures. As a result I spent most of my days in hospitals, and quickly realized just how short staffed Australia's hospitals were at the time. The doctors and nurses I worked with spent massive hours in high stress environments, and I often heard them complaining about the lack of other professionals (mainly other doctors and nurses) in the system.

I saw an opportunity in this and I wanted to do something to help fix this problem. My idea revolved around the recruitment of doctors and nurses which my research indicated to be a very profitable undertaking.

Working for an organization that didn't fit my personality was the perfect excuse for me to resign my job and pursue my next business venture with full speed! There was however one glitch in my plans to start a medical recruitment agency. Although I researched the idea quite thoroughly, I still didn't know where to begin and knew nothing about the medical recruitment process. This was a dilemma that I solved in a very cheeky way - I applied for jobs working as a recruitment consultant at an existing agency. The search didn't take long and before I knew it I was learning the ropes in a new environment. I took a huge pay cut with this job but figured it was a risk worth taking. In my head, I thought I would only need a few months before setting out on my own.

Shortly after starting it became quickly apparent to me that it was a much more serious and complicated industry than I had ever expected. Luckily I had a strong medical background so had no issues with the medical terminology. What made it complicated were the specific registration processes and requirements that involved several government agencies, non government medical bodies and a variety of overseas entities.

To make it even more complex the majority of doctors were coming from overseas, creating a phenomenal trail of paperwork that often lasted months to complete. Aside from the actual registration, I was also involved in assisting with visas and helping a doctors' family move from a foreign country to Australia. As a result of all the red tape it was no surprise that doctors turned to agencies for assistance. It was also this process that was the reason behind the lucrative nature of the industry.

To be able to explain the business itself, you have to first understand a little bit about the industry.

Within the medical recruitment game there are two main divisions:

1. Permanent – recruiting full time posts.
2. Locum – recruiting for temporary, short term or contract posts.

Within these there are further sub categories:

1. Specialists – recruiting specialist qualification holding doctors such as surgeons.
2. General practitioners – recruiting fully qualified general practitioners.
3. Juniors – recruiting doctors who have graduated from university but have not finished their training.

I learnt the ropes in all of these different categories, but due to the success I had in the specialist division that's where I focused most of my time. After about 4 months I was doing quite well in my role and had learnt enough to start thinking about stepping out.

My initial plans would be to recruit doctors at all levels and build up a team such that I would remain focused on specialists and my team looked after the rest. I had also decided to focus the business solely on permanent staffing, mainly due to the different business requirements between locums and perms, and that permanent recruitment was what I had really come to grips with.

At about this time I was also noticing just how poorly the company was being managed, with a turnover rate of almost 100% in the few months I had been there. My manager at the time, Stuart (not his real name), was having serious issues with the company directors.

Getting on well with him I knew he wasn't happy - being over the age of 50 he brought with him years of experience that was being shunned from above.

One fateful day, about 5 months into my job, we both caught the lift down to get some lunch. The usual elevator banter about the weather quickly turned to our jobs and by the time I ate my sandwich we had agreed to look into going into business together. Two weeks later I handed in my resignation and a further 2 weeks later I was free again! Stuart followed suit and left about a month after me.

Our agreement was simple. Stuart invested some money and would look after the back end of the business (banks, accounting, legal, document creation etc); I would bring my knowledge and expertise and look after the front end (sales, business development, marketing, etc).

We also agreed that we would start the business from absolute scratch, not pinching anything from our previous employers.

Honeymoon Phase

In July 2007, SpindaCorp *(the real business name has been changed for privacy reasons)*, was born. Our first month focused on setting up some basic backend documentation, banking, insurances, company logos, website and much more. In fact, these activities continued for many many more months to come. I also spent time and energy getting some adverts up on Australian and International job sites.

This period in the medical recruitment industry, although regulated, still allowed for several agencies to successfully survive. The fees we charged varied up to $30,000 per doctor, with payment by our clients made predominantly at the time the employment contract was signed by the candidate. In some cases clients negotiated to pay over 3 installments, with each installment representing the completion of an important step. From a timeframe point of view things were quite workable, with placements and documentation taking 2-4 weeks for junior doctors, 2-12 weeks for GPs and around 3-6 months for specialists. Although they were lengthy timeframes, the high fees ensured we could run our business without too many cashflow problems (especially with split payments).

The real work of recruitment started in month 2, at which point in time I got to work sourcing vacancies around the country and scouting candidates. We started strong and only 8 weeks after opening our doors I successfully placed a husband and wife specialist team for a huge fee of $60,000. We were now officially in business!

My passion for life and business had returned again. I threw myself into a 7 day week, often working 20 hours a day and enjoying every minute!

I really went above and beyond with the first two placements, an important tactic that I was using to help me secure the loyalty of my clients. Giving clients exceptional service opened them up to me and allowed me insight into what they thought of my competitors and even how my competitors operated. This was invaluable information that I used to my advantage. By gaining their trust and asking the right questions, I was able to learn the following about my competitors:

- Their pricing structure.

- How they operated.

- Information about their consultants – who was good, who wasn't.

- What they did poorly and what they did well.

With this knowledge I quickly worked out a pricing point that clients were happy with, and modified operations to make our competitors' weaknesses an obvious strength of ours, allowing us to stand out from the rest.

I didn't stop searching for more candidates and clients after making these initial two placements. I created lists of hospitals and other medical facilities from all over Australia and spent days glued to the phone, making cold call after cold call, networking amongst potential clients and building an extensive contacts list. If I am being honest with you, I might as well tell you a secret: I hate cold calling! It took me a while to get confident in this 'dark art', and even after years of practice I still don't like doing it. Having said this, cold calling is an essential tool in establishing or sourcing the first few clients of a young business (information on cold calling can be found in the Lessons on Sales and Customer Relationship Management chapter). And so, I will continue using this as part of my arsenal of sales tools, knowing full well its benefits.

Just a few months after launch I made a couple more placements and I decided it was time to get out into the marketplace, meet my clients and get to know the facilities to which I was recruiting for. I drove several thousand km's in the space of two or so weeks, met over a dozen potential clients and really took the time to understand their needs and wants. The outcome of this effort was well worth the trip, and as a result we had a tremendous first year, with invoiced revenue of several hundred thousand dollars, a strong pipeline and a number of very successful placements. I was drawing an adequate salary and had a very good working relationship with my business partner. I knew that the growth of the business was predominantly due to my efforts (all of the revenue in the first year was closed by me) and I also knew that the hours I worked were significantly higher than Stuart's. This however didn't worry me at the time, he had invested his hard earned money into the business and I figured that given a year or two he too will be busy, managing our team of consultants.

Growth Phase

I really enjoyed this first year, and with success coming so quickly we decided to bite the bullet and put on our first two staff about 10 months after starting. Both were experienced recruiters I had previously worked with, making it easy for them to step in and run with their roles.

While I had become ridiculously busy, this move to put on staff only 10 months after starting up should have waited several more months. Without realizing, I was making the same mistake of growing the business too quickly that I made with Goby. In hindsight we should have first analysed our work load and spread the tasks out more evenly with the goal of creating better work flow efficiencies. This would have enabled us to take on more work without the need for extra hands. The problem was that with the increasing number of candidates coming through and requiring processing, I had a greater and greater workload on my shoulders. This created a big discrepancy between Stuart's workload and mine, leading to frustration and annoyance on my part. I simply didn't want to rock the boat however, so I just internalized my frustrations and true feelings. It would have been smarter to hold off recruiting my own staff, but given the situation and the plans I had for SpindaCorp, it seemed like a good decision at the time to go ahead with it.

Prior to staff coming onboard our overheads were minimal, and our profit margins were large. Unlike Goby where I had massive costs related to stock, logistics and so on, with SpindaCorp I really only had costs associated with advertising and general company running expenses; recruitment is an industry where a simple laptop and mobile phone are adequate enough to run a successful agency. With technology offering so much in the way of flexibility, we decided that at least for the first few years we would not move into a dedicated office, but would have all staff and ourselves set up at home, dialing into a dedicated company server to keep track of all work. This helped keep our overheads low, but as you will later read, running and managing a team of remotely working consultants proved a challenging task.

As I just mentioned before, one would think that I would have learnt my lesson from the Goby days and not grow the company so rapidly without adequate resources. With two experienced consultants now on our team, the workload coming through the company literally doubled within two months of them starting! It was fantastic being this busy, and gave me a false sense of security that we were going to succeed in a big way. The cost of carrying the two new staff was a burden for the first month, but we got a lucky break weeks after their commencement as both successfully closed contracts and brought in enough revenue to cover their costs for the coming month or two. The overall profit margin was significantly impacted due to the cost of having staff join us, but we had every intention of getting them to bill at least triple what they cost the business. This however would take a year to achieve, a reality we didn't really consider.

As the 1st quarter of our second year came to an end we had so much work coming in that we saw no option but to put on 3 more full time staff, including a personal assistant to help me out with my work.

With SpindaCorp now consisting of 5 full time staff plus Stuart and I only 15 months after opening doors, it was becoming more of a struggle for us to maintain the strong profit margins we had in the beginning. Our overheads went up dramatically with the cost of maintaining five permanent staff, and our cash in the bank took a beating. Although there was a lot of work on the table, it would take 3-6 months before a consultant was billing enough consistently to cover all of their costs to the company, and until then the costs were our responsibility. Unfortunately we didn't factor this appropriately into our budgets or forecasts and as a result we ended up having to carry more costs than planned.

Had all of our clients agreed to upfront payments we would have had no issues, but the industry was changing and clients were becoming very reluctant to pay agency fees upfront. Most were opting to pay us in three installments, which meant lengthy periods before we saw any money come in from assignments, and thus we were having to carry larger expenses for much longer periods. Due to this combination, around 18 months into the business we ended up having to resort to an overdraft account to sail us through while payments came in. At the time though, this did not worry me too much. The first quarter was very strong for us and I was confident we could keep the level of activity high.

This confidence paid off a few months later and we ended the first half of our 2nd year on a massive high. We had an incredible past 6 months, so much so that as a team our combined placements were worth well over double what our first year revenue was! We were now well on our way to hitting my personal goal: smashing $1 million in invoiced revenue for the 2nd year in business.

Again though, despite the amount of contracts being signed, money was taking a long time to get to us due to the timeframes of the payment agreements. It was a risk that previously posed little threat as we expected almost all of our placements to go to completion, allowing us to realize the full fee for the assignment.

Beginning of the End

Unfortunately for us, halfway through our 2nd year in business two major events occurred that significantly impacted on SpindaCorp, our industry and business globally.

1. The ramifications of the Global Financial Crisis (GFC) became apparent in more and more countries, causing market nervousness, volatility and a changing political arena. For us this was bad news. The vast majority of our doctors were from overseas (especially specialists of whom 100% were foreign trained), and the majority of our candidates were coming from countries that took a battering from the GFC. Property markets tumbled, business confidence diminished and many of our candidates were simply stuck as they couldn't move forward without selling their assets. Others were taken aback by the global happenings and decided to put on hold plans to move until things settled down again.

2. If the GFC wasn't enough, overseas trained doctors (OTD's) working in Australia were now more in the spotlight than ever before. As a result of the immense public pressure and negative media publicity that resulted from a couple of high profile cases, government bureaucrats turned up the heat and the red tape drastically thickened. Procedures and selection criteria tightened, paperwork increased and timeframes around registrations and visas significantly grew. If that wasn't enough, several

major international newspapers published articles depicting Australians as racist and unjust. The impact of all of this on our business was frustrating and painful.

No sooner had the 3rd quarter begun, the above two issues had made themselves very real to us. Of the 8 specialists I placed in the first 6 months of the year (worth $288,000), all but 2 pulled out. My team experienced the same and a large portion of the contracts we had on the go fell over. The doctors all said the same thing: it was too risky for them to move in such unsettling global times, when it was almost impossible for them to even sell their homes in their respective countries. They were also concerned of the news they heard from other overseas doctors already in Australia about the way they were being treated by the Government and medical boards.

Apart from the financial issues, I was having issues with staff and Stuart. The work from home arrangement worked for a small amount of time but I learnt that very few people are really cut out for working in such isolated conditions. Most made a good start, but fizzled out after a few short weeks, leaving me to constantly be on their backs about their workloads, which simply drained team morale in the process. Without a team constantly around to motivate them, some really struggled. As a result, I lost two staff in quarter 3.

The issues with Stuart were more complex. As the team grew in numbers I was expecting him to step up more and really get hands on, providing coaching and leading by example. Unfortunately this did not occur and I found myself also taking on this role. My team was disgruntled with his management style, and at one point all of them complained to me about Stuart and his ways. A common theme was occurring: he was pushing the team to perform, but apart from delegating and micromanaging they did not see him doing anything else. I kept covering for him for several months and not tackling the problem, but the straw finally broke and I had to sit down with him in order to air the issues.

Following a very heated discussion we settled down and came up with a mutually agreed solution. We identified the key roles within the business and divvied up the workload – a move that in hindsight should have been done much sooner. We also agreed that moving forward no issues would be kept stewing, creating instead an open atmosphere for communication.

For a short while things settled down between us and our arrangement worked. It wasn't long though before we were having more and more arguments about the business, especially on the financial side of things.

Topping it all off, stresses put on the business from external forces was growing day by day, and virtually every few weeks something was changing with the process of medical registration. It was now becoming quite a challenge to source overseas trained doctors whom we were confident not only had the right qualifications and experience to attain a successful registration outcome, but who were prepared to commit to the grueling process. I even travelled overseas to source candidates directly, an expensive exercise which proved fruitless.

By the middle of 2009 the registration timeframes had escalated and specialists were now taking 18-24 months to go through the full process, while overseas general practitioners were taking up to 9 months. The juniors market faced a complete change in procedures, and hospitals changed their requirements in line with this. Suffice to say this was a stressful period!

Business was suffering. It was incredibly frustrating watching bureaucrats make decisions that were so directly affecting our performance. What was most frustrating however was knowing that there was a strong demand for our services, there was demand for more doctors, we had well over 2,000 on our books yet they could not get into the system without an incredible uphill battle. If I had a significant amount of money in the bank, enough to run the business for the next 2 years, we could have come out very strong. Unfortunately though we had to make do with what we had.

Due to the financial pressures we were forced to first cut wages for ourselves, then having to cut wages for our staff as well, offering commission only arrangements. Of the three remaining consultants one resigned immediately. The other two still believed in SpindaCorp and stayed on, albeit on commission only, and we promised to put them back on a salary as soon as possible.

The financial pressures were also felt at home, with the up and down of my salary making it tough to keep going, to justify sticking with SpindaCorp.

It was amazing just how fast a business can go from nothing to boom and back down again! Looking back at the past 2 years, it was amazing how the whole sector completely shifted and changed in such a short timeframe.

Unfortunately we didn't crack the $1 million revenue in our 2nd year which I had aimed for, although we did manage to double our prior year revenue. Given our increased costs however (which was actually more than the total income for the year), our reliance on the overdraft facility grew.

By the start of the 3rd year in business the only sector that was still strong was the GP locum sector, within which we only dabbled in until now. We had little choice however, so we changed our business focus and shifted most of our efforts towards that sector. I still had a couple of ongoing specialists but I wasn't expecting any to come through. To make things worse, at this point I lost another team member.

I was determined to turn the business around and recruited two new staff to work in the locum division, on a commission only basis (one of them was actually a former client of mine). Again in hindsight this move should have waited. We had minimal setup in this division, it was basically like recruiting two staff into a new business. The smarter thing to do would have been taking this on between Stuart and I and setting it up until the work was heavy, and only then putting on staff.

Stuart and I still wanted to continue with the business as there was ample potential, but as we ran out of our own personal money and the bank overdraft was close to being maxed out, we knew our days were numbered. With limited funds for marketing and candidate sourcing, our attempt to crack the locum market was unsuccessful. I personally reached a point where I knew that if no more money comes in, I would be forced to go get another job just to survive.

Foreseeing the possibility of such an event months in advance, the beginning of our 3rd year also saw the start of our preparation to try and either merge with another agency or to sell out all together. Discussions started with a couple of prospective 'suitors', but the negotiations stalled and an agreement could not be reached that was beneficial to both parties. Towards the end of 2009 we ran out of funds and I had to start looking for another job. I resigned as a director of SpindaCorp, gave up my shares and went back into employed work after two and a half years of running SpindaCorp.

The End

The last few months between Stuart and I were not pleasant and arguments about how much we each owed and contributed to the business continued. As neither one of us wanted to go bankrupt, the only option was to pay off the overdraft facility month by month until we could each get separate loans to pay out our share. Eventually we reached an agreement after many heated conversations. The amount was huge, but better than the alternative.

It didn't take long for me to find suitable employment, allowing my wife and I to stay on top of our finances and start paying off the debt. Six months later I refinanced our house and paid out the debt owing to the business. I was finally free of the burden and ready to reflect on the past 2.5 years with SpindaCorp.

Lessons Learnt

A lot of what I learnt from my Goby days allowed me to run a significantly tighter ship with SpindaCorp. My financial understanding had come a long way, as had my leadership and general management skills. What I also learnt from my Goby days was to stay headstrong, focused, and not let myself slip into a bad mental state. As a result although it was devastating to close yet another venture, I was more realistic about it all and much more willing to learn from my mistakes (although I did make the mistake of growing too fast yet again!).

Throughout the years I have been in business I never had any real help or guidance from anyone. Even when I sought help I found it difficult to get the right advice. What I hope to achieve out of this book is to provide you with some guidance on the Realities of Business, to help you think more carefully about your actions and decisions so that you have a better chance of succeeding in your own ventures.

The next section of this book will focus on the lessons that I have learnt and will delve deeper into some of the pitfalls you need to be aware of when running your own business.

Remember, this is not a get rich guide. This book is a tool to get you thinking more realistically about business and the long term implications immediate decisions can have on the eventual success of your business. Learn from my mistakes and lessons, and use this book as a stepping stone towards further education on business – and hopefully success!

UPDATED CONTENT – January 2015

This book you are reading is the revised version of the first edition. I am a perfectionist and couldn't resist the urge to go back and update the content, add in new stuff, take out bits, rewrite bits and fiddle with the book until I was finally happy with the end result!

As I am writing this, I look at the date: 8th Jan 2015 and think to myself: sheesh, it's been almost exactly 3 years since the first edition of this book came out, and so much in my life has changed! Wow!

The story contained within the first edition ended of this book recalled my story up until the end of 2009.

Since then, a lot has changed.

Firstly, I am now a father of three young ones. That in itself has meant a massive change in my lifestyle. I can no longer work 15 hour days, 7 days a week. I can no longer take the sort of risks that I could take when such responsibility was out of the picture. Having said this, and very interestingly, my output, efficiency and results generated are higher than ever before. I am super focused on the task at hand, and given my 'limited' works hours I have to ensure that whatever I do isn't wasteful and is always in the best interest of my family.

So let's go back in time a few years.

After the demise of SpindaCorp, as mentioned earlier on in the piece, I found employed work and settled into a challenging corporate role working for a large, ASX listed company. I would like to think that I was successful in that role, but of course as it happens with any true entrepreneur, the bug to be independent and in my own business just wouldn't go away. It was actually while writing this book back in 2010/11 that I decided on my next business move: education and consulting, and so in July 2012 I made the jump once again from that of employee to self-employed, and launched my next venture, Realities of Business.

Shortly after launching I landed an ongoing contract with a fast growing marketing agency, which enabled me to hone and develop my products and processes. At the end of the contract I successfully built my client base thanks mainly to word of mouth and partner referrals, and I have been running Realities of Business ever since.

Of course, as with all businesses, I have had ups and downs with this one too, and there have certainly been challenges that I had previously not encountered. Being a consulting firm, clients often have incorrectly predisposed ideas about how it all works and how the results would pan out. This led to friction in a few cases, and even resulted in me walking away from some clients. You know what though? Sometimes in business it is better to walk away relatively amicably from clients, then to try and argue points and prove your clients wrong, or trying to 'massage' something until it is completely bastardized in order to fit the special needs of a client. It's just not worth the fight in the long run! This can be hard to do though, especially when you know you are in the right...

Other than a few hiccups, overall the business has done very well and is actually now in a new phase of evolution, which I will touch on shortly.

Along the journey of Realities of Business, many of my clients required services beyond consulting, which I initially outsourced to third party providers. This however turned into a nightmare as the third party providers time and again stuffed up the work and caused more headaches than anyone had anticipated. So, I took matters into my own hands and I expanded on my initial consulting services. Soon enough I was providing a range of implementation services to help clients get better results from their business, and was starting to make more money from those services than the original consulting services I started with.

Being well received by the market, in late 2013 I decided to spin off a new company dedicated to implementation services such as website development and online marketing. This new venture, Digital Duet (www.digitalduet.com.au), was launched in January 2014.

So now I have 2 businesses up and running, providing services ranging from consulting through to digital marketing solutions and more (check out my websites www.digitalduet.com.au and www.peterspinda.com). As I write this update, 12 months on from starting Digital Duet, the business is definitely gaining momentum, and the hours and hours of work I had initially put into the setup of this business has paid off in the form of good productivity and good client results. I won't go into much more detail about Digital Duet just yet, it needs time to stabilize and mature as a business - perhaps in a future revision you will read a full chapter (or perhaps a whole new book) on the great success (or not) that I had with this venture! And should you need web development or online marketing services or even help setting up a business, you know who to turn to!

And in terms of Realities of Business? Well, as I said before it is evolving. All of my consulting work has been moved to Digital Duet, and Realities of Business is being turned into a provider of real world business education workshops, seminars and online courses. This will take some time however to achieve.....

What the future holds for me and my current businesses is unknown.

All I can say is that some days, I just want to stay in bed and not get up.

Other days, the sun is shining, birds are chirping and gold is glistening!

And you know what? **These are the Realities of Business!**

No matter how long you have been at it, no matter how much knowledge you have accumulated, there are always going to be days when you wonder why you bother. Days when you want to give up. Days when crying and curling up in a little ball seem like the only option.

When that occurs to you, and trust me, IT WILL, just remember this little saying that I have and KEEP GOING:

'Success is the product of one's ability to learn from failure'.

Inspired: , left, and Peter Spinda — virtual-bookshop entrepreneurs   Picture: Jeremy Piper

Text prices drive up ingenuity

Daniel Hoare

FED up with paying high prices for textbooks, two student entrepreneurs have taken things into their own hands and set up a website dedicated to selling higher education resources.

The new web business, www.goby.com.au, is an expanded version of the site www.gethealthy.com.au, which Peter Spinda and established two years ago in response to the spiralling cost of textbooks and medical equipment for health science students.

Its stock includes such items as giant eyes, brains in eight parts and acupuncture charts.

Spinda and , both 22-year-old chiropractic students at Macquarie University, will launch the virtual bookshop on Saturday, offering more than 1 million books aimed at university and TAFE-students Australia-wide.

The entrepreneurs reckon they haven't looked back since snaffling a range of IT and e-commerce textbooks and launching the site. "Everything that's been done up to this point has been done by us. We learnt everything ourselves, all the coding, all the HTML, everything," said Spinda.

The business has absorbed about $80,000 but Spinda says it is trading in the black ahead of the launch of the new site.

Above: The article published by The Australian newspaper upon the launch of the Goby website.

www.GOBY.com.au

Left: The Goby logo

Above: My first ever business card.

Left: Pietro Gregori was my own men's fashion label. This is a sample of the tie and cufflink sets I had manufactured and branded for me.

Notice to Students

Textbooks now available online at highly reduced prices.

Minimum 20% OFF RRP ALL Textbooks!

Receive **FREE** shipping,
FREE membership
and
FREE stuff with your first order!

www.GOBY.com.au

'run by students, for students'

NO CREDIT CARDS REQUIRED

Above: An example of a Goby flyer that I pasted all over University campuses.

SECTION 2

Real business lessons.

REALITIES

My story and my experiences in business are not unusual. Talk to any business owner and they will no doubt be able to recall times of difficulty, times when they didn't know what the next day will bring. They will also tell you of the good times, when success is at their door and things are looking up.

The harsh reality you must come to terms with is that most businesses will fail in the first few years of existence. The reasons they fail are as diverse as the types of businesses out there. From poor management to bad ideas that should never have been pursued, sometimes failure is our own making. Other times though, it can all be out of our control. The Global Financial Crisis of recent years is a prime example of what can happen when market sentiment turns sour, affecting virtually everybody and every business.

In any case, if you prepare yourself, up skill and learn from past mistakes (be it your own or others), you will be in a better position to succeed.

My observation of other businesses and my own experience in business has made me realize that the majority of businesses follow a life cycle similar to the image below:

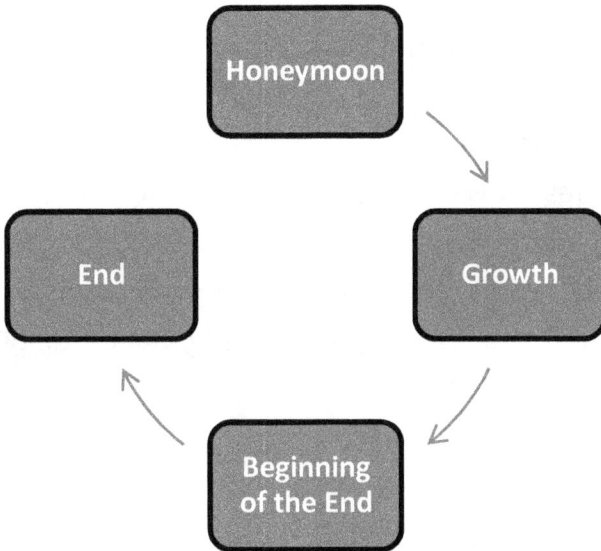

This is a very simplified diagram I know, but later on in the book I will talk about this cycle in more detail, as well as how you can develop your business so that it doesn't end up in this cycle.

So, looking at the cycle, here is what happens in far too many cases:

The period from when the individual starts thinking about starting a new venture, through to the execution and the first few months in business is always very exciting. This is what I call the Honeymoon Phase. In this phase the individual often dreams of where their idea would take them, and more often than not throws themselves into the business with as much enthusiasm and energy as a child that has been given the keys to a chocolate shop! After a few months in business, the realities of their venture would start surfacing. As their procedures develop into standard daily tasks and revenue now regularly comes in, they entered what I call the Growth Phase. For me this was always an incredibly busy period that focused on building the business both externally and internally. Unfortunately for most business owners, the growth phase (if they even get to that phase) is followed by a downturn in business and a period I call the Beginning of the End. This is the period that leads up to the end of the business – a critical phase that all too often leads to the collapse of the business, and an overall intensely challenging time from a personal perspective.

The reason I point this out to you is simple: the sad reality is that the vast majority of businesses go through a similar cycle. Being aware of this however will better prepare you for what may lie ahead – and as you will learn, you can use the challenging periods to fuel a resurgence in order to avoid the crash.

Within each of these phases lie its own set of challenges that require you to utilize and learn new skills. The following sections will look at some of the key lessons I learnt throughout the lifecycle of my businesses, and will hopefully give you a realistic insight into the running of a business.

Lessons on Personal Development

Life is like a river for many people, they just jump in the river of life without ever deciding where they want to end up, so they quickly get caught up in the current: current events, current challenges, and current fears. Then they come to the forks in the rivers; they don't consciously decide which way to go, they just go with the flow of the river (the flow of the majority instead of being directed by their own values and goals) and as a result they feel out of control, but continue to drift downstream until one day the sound of the raging water wakes them up and they realize they are 5 feet from the falls and they are in a boat with no oars and then they say "Oh shoot", but it's too late. They are going to take a fall. It may be a financial setback or the breakup of a relationship or maybe even a health problem. In almost all of the cases however, the fall could have been prevented by making better decisions upstream. - Anthony Robbins.

Deciding to go into business for yourself is a very exciting step. Like most entrepreneurs, even ones who have gone through several ventures, there is no doubt that throughout your business journey you will catch yourself thinking about business success and what it will mean for you. Perhaps you see yourself driving a brand new sports car. Maybe you see yourself retiring young and travelling the world doing whatever you want to do. Whatever it is that you wish to achieve, making your dreams a reality will subject you to not only a myriad of business challenges, but to a whole raft of personal ones too.

Beware the Dreamers Trap!

All too often I hear of people who had come up with an idea which in their minds was the best idea ever, but then they fail miserably when it comes time to implement and bring the idea to reality.

Mistakes are easy to make: All too often occurring when the dreamer's idealistic thoughts combine with inexperience and a hastened, rushed attitude. I am very guilty of this and have caused myself serious grief and headache on numerous occasions simply by rushing into things without a well thought out plan in place. Just look at how I approached Goby – I was totally unrealistic about my goals and expectations, and spent more time worrying about the future and dreaming of making millions than being in the present and taking the slow, strategic road.

Before you even start thinking about business ideas, it is important that you get yourself into a goal oriented, dream driven but realistic mindset. Doing this will enable you to dream big, whilst always keeping your feet firmly on the ground, acutely aware of the realities around you.

I entered my first business only with the dreamers mind and was caught off guard. The result of this was a raft of costly, silly mistakes that could have been avoided. Lesson learnt, I changed my attitude with SpindaCorp.

Before I even worked on the idea for that business I did 3 things:

1. Understood my exact financial position. I looked at my expenses, my savings and worked out how long I could afford to not receive an income should I go ahead with the idea on a full time basis. I also looked at how much I could invest into the business, knowing full well that I may never again see one cent of whatever I put in.

2. I learnt more about my personality. I looked at:

- My strengths

- My weaknesses

- How I handle stress and pressure

- Where I want to go in life

- Why I want to go into business

3. I looked back at my first business and reminded myself of what it really meant to run a business. As a dreamer all I saw was that I would sell books and make a profit. In reality however this becomes much more complicated, since running a business will require you to learn and utilize skills in:

- Idea development

- Business planning

- Financial management

- Marketing and branding

- Sales and customer management

- Negotiation

- Staff management

- And so much more!

Knowing and being aware of the above from the onset will help you with decision making processes, and will give you an early indication of whether a potential venture is really suited to you. So now it's your turn. Grab a pen and paper, and following the 3 points I outline above I want you to put yourself through this exercise. Seriously. Do it – **NOW!**

Let's be honest – business is tough. Apart from the need to understand how to manage and grow a business, you also have to prepare yourself mentally for the challenges ahead, to give you the strength and stamina needed to push through tough times. As you go through the process of getting to know yourself and becoming confident with yourself and your personality, you will hopefully start seeing and approaching business ideas with a greater understanding of what is and isn't realistic for you. There is a lot to be gained simply by understanding who you really are.

Looking back at my two businesses, it is now very clear to me why I didn't crumble when SpindaCorp failed. First of all, I was well prepared mentally for anything that could come up (in fact, I had a failure plan in mind from day one – the last chapter goes into this in detail). Second, and very importantly, my family and friends supported me with SpindaCorp.

Support

When times were tough during the days of SpindaCorp, my wife would always listen to me and would give me the strength I needed to keep going. My parents, brother and friends were also always there to support me. Goby on the other hand was different. As that business was failing, so was a long term relationship I was in. On top of that, I lacked the support I truly needed from my family and friends. Not because they didn't care, but because they didn't understand what I was going through. My friends were all young university students who thought working 10 hours a week at a fast food joint was stressful, and I felt too ashamed to talk honestly and openly about my feelings with my family.

Consequently, I discovered that for me, having a strong support network is invaluable in business and in life.

Don't Stop Dreaming!

Although I am a believer of tackling a new business venture on a realistic level, I still firmly believe that you need to keep setting yourself high goals and dreaming of big things. Don't settle for anything but the best outcome with your business, and keep striving to achieve the goals you set yourself. Keep dreaming, keep closing your eyes at night and imagining what it will be like when your dreams are a reality. Just make sure you do this with your feet firmly on the ground, aware of the heartbeat of your business, aware of the realities surrounding your venture. Use your dreams and goals as the fuel to propel you and your business forward with enthusiasm and energy.

Lewis Carroll's famous masterpiece 'Through the Looking Glass' (the sequel to Alice's Adventures in Wonderland) contains a story that exemplifies the need to dream the impossible dream. There is a conversation between Alice and the queen, which goes like this:

"I can't believe that!" said Alice.

"Can't you?" the queen said in a pitying tone. "Try again, draw a long breath, and shut your eyes."

Alice laughed. "There's no use trying," she said. "One can't believe impossible things."

"I dare say you haven't had much practice," said the queen. "When I was your age, I always did it for half an hour a day. Why, sometimes I've believed as many as six impossible things before breakfast."

Dare to dream and magic can happen!

Lessons on Idea Development

The 3M Company encourages creativity from its employees. The company allows its researchers to spend 15 percent of their time on any project that interests them. This attitude has brought fantastic benefits not only to the employees but to the 3M Company itself. Many times, a spark of an idea turned into a successful product has boosted 3M's profits tremendously.

Some years ago, a scientist in 3M's commercial office took advantage of this 15 percent creative time. This scientist, Art Fry, came up with an idea for one of 3M's best-selling products. It seems that Art Fry dealt with a small irritation every Sunday as he sang in the church choir. After marking his pages in the hymnal with small bits of paper, the small pieces would invariably fall out all over the floor.

Suddenly, an idea struck Fry. He remembered an adhesive developed by a colleague that everyone thought was a failure because it did not stick very well. "I coated the adhesive on a paper sample," Fry recalls, "and I found that it was not only a good bookmark, but it was great for writing notes. It will stay in place as long as you want it to, and then you can remove it without damage." And so, Post-it! Notes were born. Source: 3M Company.

I have a Dream

All businesses start out life as an idea that eventually turns into reality. Ideas that turn into successful businesses usually do so as a result of a combination of 2 main reasons, with luck sometimes playing an important part:

1. Good idea
2. Good execution

Although I got lucky with my first idea (having jumped straight into it without much preparation), luck can only take you so far, as demonstrated by the eventual demise of that initially successful business.

Putting luck aside, it is important to understand that unless you take control of your idea and undertake appropriate due diligence, you significantly increase your chances of stepping into a venture that is doomed from the beginning.

Before we jump the gun though and start talking about turning an idea into a real business, let's take a few steps back and look at how you can come up with your own business ideas, followed by looking at how you analyze and develop an idea to ensure that it is a viable idea from all angles.

Coming up with Ideas

For me, the easiest aspect of developing a business idea has always been coming up with the actual idea. There are potential opportunities all around you – just become a keen observer of your surroundings and learn to recognize a need from your observations. This need is a problem for someone – the business or idea is the solution to that problem. I'll give you a few of my own examples:

1. **Observation:** Purchasing textbooks from a physical shop was a hassle. It was time consuming and required me to travel to a physical shop when I had better things to do.

   Idea: Sell books online.

2. **Observation:** Good quality silk ties and nice cufflinks can be very expensive. Cheap ones are often of a poor quality and design.

   Idea: Sell good quality ties and cufflinks at affordable prices.

3. **Observation:** Hospitals severely lack medical staff.

Idea: Recruit doctors to come and work in Australia.

4. **Observation:** Traditional syringes pose a potential threat of needle stick injuries to not only users, but the general public. Despite this, there was no other alternative in the Australian market to the traditional syringe.

   Idea: Source syringes that eliminate this issue.

5. **Observation:** Many so called web development and online marketing companies lack good business processes and customer service.

   Idea: Setup my own digital solutions company.

To further enhance your skills in spotting business ideas, I also suggest that you learn to recognize key words and sentences in communication. These include:

- Sentences that start with 'Why', e.g. Why can't they make this easier.

- Sentences starting with: If only; I wish.

- Statements that indicate towards a better solution, e.g. I could do this better myself.

Armed with your idea/s the process of idea analysis and elimination can begin. This process is important for the following reasons:

1. Ensures that the really good idea in your head is also good in reality.

2. Ensures that the idea that is good in reality is suitable for you and your circumstances.

3. Helps you personally prepare for the realities and challenges that will lie ahead.

4. You will find that there is nothing that boosts your energy and enthusiasm more in the beginning of a venture than having confidence that your idea can truly become successful!

Apart from my 4 main businesses and a couple of small projects, I have gone through dozens of ideas that in my head were great, but were either not viable at the time, too complicated/costly to execute or simply not possible with my available knowledge and resources. Many of these were very simplistic ideas at first glance, but trust me when I say that **simplicity is complexity in disguise**.

Take note of this advice:

Even the simplest of ideas are complicated and challenging to execute

Standing in the bookshop line all those years ago, I thought that the idea of selling textbooks online would be a very simple process. I would purchase goods for $x, sell for $y and make profit $z. I would be making money on my own terms, working part time on the business, whilst I was studying. Looking back now, it is amazing how underprepared I was and even more amazing that the business took off and survived for as long as it did!

Just how underprepared and unrealistic I was is best demonstrated in the diagrams on the following page.

This was my view when I first started Goby:

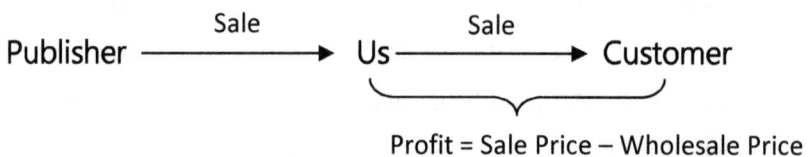

Publisher $\xrightarrow{\text{Sale}}$ Us $\xrightarrow{\text{Sale}}$ Customer

Profit = Sale Price – Wholesale Price

I really didn't think there was any more to it than that. In reality however this is what happened:

Negotiating Accounts
Managing Invoices
Placing Orders
Warehousing

Packaging
Shipping
Marketing
Complains Management

Publisher ⟶ Us ⟶ Customer

Business Management:
- Taxation
- Paperwork
- Financial Management
- Business Development
- Staff Management

Website Management
Refunds
Transaction Management
Invoicing
Debt Collection

Profit = Sale Price – (Wholesale Price + Transaction Processing Costs + a portion of all business related expenses)

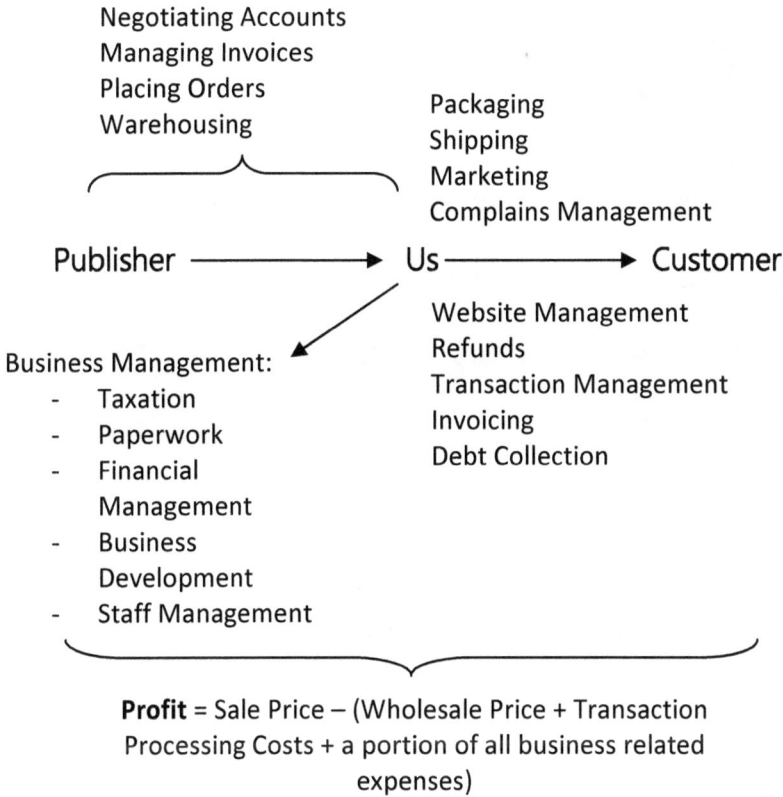

As you can see from the above, there is more to rolling out a business idea and running a business than looking at how much money you could make out of it.

In fact there are quite a few factors that will affect the realistic potential of your ideas:

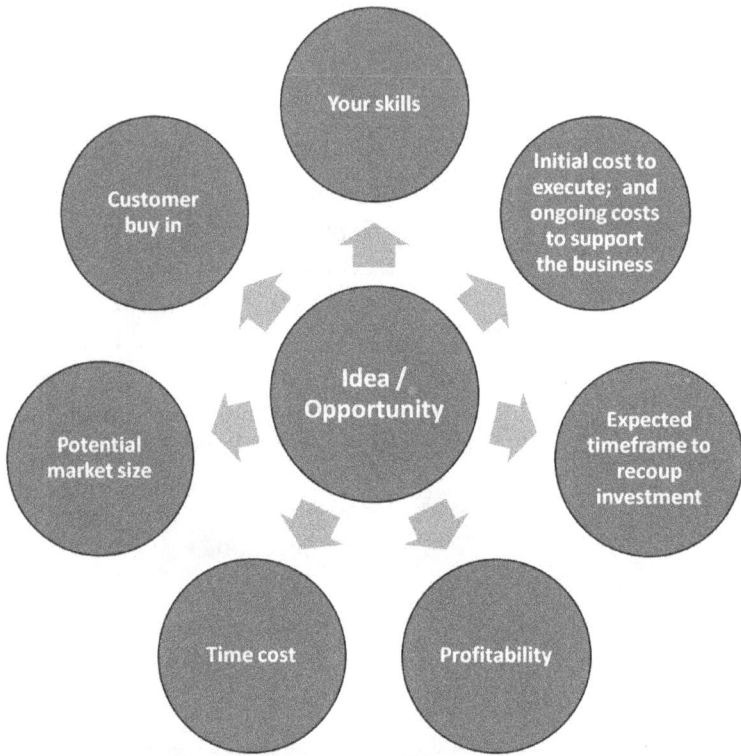

So how do you know if your idea has legs and how do you take the step from dream to reality?

Analyzing your Ideas

Referring back to the above diagram, when I look at the viability of an idea I spend time researching the answers to a set of questions that will either tell me not to bother further with the idea, or prompt me to continue my research and look at devising an execution strategy to bring the idea to life.

The questionnaire below is a good starting point to help you identify ideas that you could potentially turn into businesses.

Idea questionnaire

- What is the idea?
- Does the idea already exist as a business?
- If yes, why should you still consider this idea?
- What will differentiate your idea from other similar businesses?
- If the idea doesn't exist, how do you know there is a market in it?
- What is the potential market size for this business?
- Do you have the skills, contacts and resources (this includes money, time etc.) to bring the idea to life and turn it into a viable business?
- If no, how will you fill any voids (e.g. raise funds)?
- What will it cost to turn your idea into reality (include all relevant expenses)?
- What will it cost to run such a business once you have executed the idea?
- Where will the money come from to cover this?

- How long after launching your idea are you expecting to generate revenue?
- How long will it take to recoup your investment?
- Can you afford to have this amount tied up so long?
- What are your plans should the idea take longer than expected to take off and requires further injection of capital?
- Can you afford to lose your investment?
- What is this potential opportunity worth?
- What is your anticipated profit margin?
- Will you need to commit all your time to this, i.e. quit your job or will it be part time initially?
- If part time, will this enable you to commit enough time and energy to adequately launch your idea?

It has taken me several years, with a number of mistakes along the way, to learn how to proficiently and quickly analyze ideas and validate them as being realistic and possible. Practice this questionnaire frequently and you will no doubt quickly realize just how powerful this process really is. I have applied a similar line of questioning to dozens of ideas over the years with only a handful proving to be a viable option so far.

The answers to some of these questions may be the same for all ideas, especially around the available money and time. In some cases however, even these may change. For example, I was willing to give up my job and risk everything for SpindaCorp; however, when I setup my own tie brand I was initially only willing to invest a few hours per week, and I only had a fraction of the money to invest compared to that of SpindaCorp.

It may take some time before an idea/opportunity presents itself that you find worthwhile pursuing. Once you have that idea though you are ready to take the step closer to reality!

Lessons on Business Planning and Launching Your Idea

A singing bird was confined in a cage which hung outside a window, and had a way of singing at night when all other birds were asleep. One night a Bat came and clung to the bars of the cage, and asked the Bird why she was silent by day and sang only at night. "I have a very good reason for doing so," said the Bird. "It was once when I was singing in the daytime that a fowler was attracted by my voice, and set his nets for me and caught me. Since then I have never sung except by night." But the Bat replied, "It is no use you doing that now when you are a prisoner: if only you had done so before you were caught, you might still have been free."

"Precautions are useless after the crisis" – Aesop.

The Execution Map

Having identified a business idea that could be worth pursuing, your next few steps will revolve around the creation of a strategy to bring your idea to reality. This is an important step, for it will give you a deeper understanding of the realities surrounding your idea, potentially preventing you from jumping head first into a dead venture. In fact, it may well be that during this process you decide that the idea isn't worth pursuing any further and you go back to the drawing board to look for more suitable business options.

Very Important Note: If you can't make an idea work on paper then chances are you will seriously struggle bringing it to life. Don't be afraid to ditch ideas that you are unsure about – there is no point gambling your money on an uncertainty; you are better off starting your research again and spending your time and money on ideas that prove to have greater potential, and are realistically viable.

As a first step, it is imperative that you get a better understanding of the realities surrounding your idea. Some of the questions you need answered at this stage are:

- What will executing my idea actually entail?

- What back end work will I need to do to get it off the ground?

- How involved will this process be?

- How much money and time will I need?

- Based on all of the available information, is it still an idea I should pursue?

To get a good understanding of the realities around your idea I recommend you create a mind map similar to the one below:

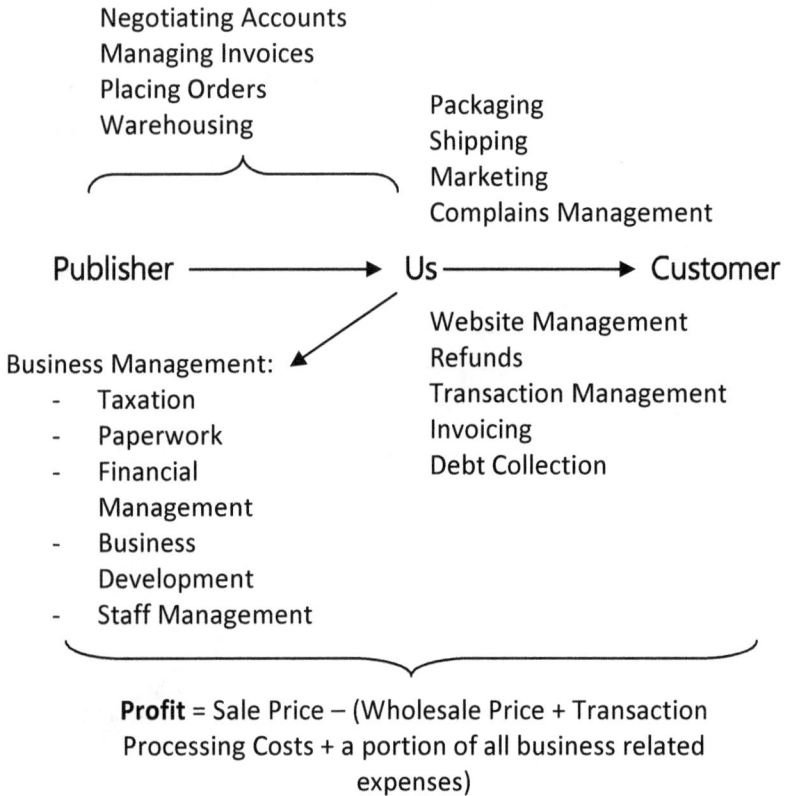

Negotiating Accounts
Managing Invoices
Placing Orders
Warehousing

Packaging
Shipping
Marketing
Complains Management

Publisher ⟶ Us ⟶ Customer

Business Management:
- Taxation
- Paperwork
- Financial Management
- Business Development
- Staff Management

Website Management
Refunds
Transaction Management
Invoicing
Debt Collection

Profit = Sale Price − (Wholesale Price + Transaction Processing Costs + a portion of all business related expenses)

When creating this map bear in mind the following:

- The purpose of your map is to help you identify the steps needed in order to take your idea off the page and turn it into a viable business.

- All businesses have three angles: one that your customers can see, one that your suppliers can see, and one that only you can see. You need to ensure that all of these three angles are covered in your execution map.

Looking at your three business angles:

1. **Customer Angle** – This is the interaction your business has with the customer, where the transaction occurs. Questions to consider (and I am sure you will come up with many more yourself!):

    a. How will they come to hear of you?

    b. How will you sell them your products or services?

    c. How will you handle product or service issues?

    d. How will they pay you?

    e. How will you market to them on an ongoing basis?

    f. How will you handle negative publicity?

2. **Your Angle** – This is the back end management of your business. Questions to consider:

   a. What forms and documentation do you need to run your business (e.g. invoice books etc.)?

   b. What bank accounts, merchant accounts, accountants, book keepers etc. need to be organized?

   c. What suppliers or business service providers do you need?

   d. Is your product or service ready in its current form to be presented to the market place?

   e. Have you got your financial management documentation sorted?

3. **Supplier Angle** – This is the interaction your business has with suppliers (whether they be product or service providers).

   a. Do you have all of the relevant supplier contacts you need in order to be able to run your business?

b. Do you know what relevant wholesale/distribution agreements you will need?

c. Have you considered your logistics channels?

d. Have you got your ordering and payments processes sorted?

I used a similar execution map for when I set up SpindaCorp, Realities of Business and Digital Duet, and found it invaluable. Having a clear understanding of what the running of the business required, I had a good overview of what I needed to do to get to the stage where I could actually launch that business in the marketplace. The execution map also forms a good base for the next step, which is the creation of your business plan.

Your Business Plan

If you have gone through all of the above and you are still keen on your idea, there is only one more step left before you can get working on breathing life into the idea. Using your execution map as a guide, let's now focus on creating your business plan.

I have written numerous business plans over the years, some for my companies, others as part of my role working for someone else. The one thing I have learnt from spending countless hours poring over figures and analyzing and researching data is that a 100 page business plan with well laid out charts and numerous financial spreadsheets is absolutely useless, and a complete waste of time, unless the document is regularly utilized as part of your business process. Don't overcomplicate things. As long as it contains the right information, a business plan does not need to be hundreds of pages long.

The initial purpose of the plan is to assist you in **bringing your idea to life** by identifying the key processes and steps that need to be completed prior to and post business launch. Once your business is operational, the purpose of the business plan is to then **help guide the growth of your business**. If used regularly, your business plan will naturally evolve and grow with your business, helping you constantly be aware of any potential dangers ahead, identifying new areas of opportunity, and helping with the smooth running of your operations.

Now, grab your execution map from before, you will need it to help create your business plan.

Suggested content for your business plan:

- An outline of your idea
- An outline of funding options including:
    - Initial investment amount
    - Source of funds
    - Repayment timeframes
- Create a financial snapshot of your business, outlining expenses, revenue and 1st year Earnings Before Interest and Tax.
- A discussion around the basic setup requirements, including:
    - Registering business names and obtaining relevant business numbers
    - Taxation and banking etc.
    - Information such as timeframes to complete by and cost to complete (where relevant)
- Requirements specific to your idea:
    - Look at what you need to do to make your product or service ready for market – e.g. sourcing suppliers, manufacturers etc.
    - How will you interact with customers and what do you need to do to set this up – e.g. shop front – arrange lease; online presence – website creation etc.

- o What will the above cost?
- Marketing:
    - o How will your customers hear of your business and your products/services?
    - o What will your brand look like? What will it stand for?
    - o What will marketing cost?
- Logistics:
    - o How do you plan to get products to customers?
    - o Map out your logistics channel including the supply chain from your suppliers to you, and from you to your customers.
    - o Don't forget that logistics incorporates: warehousing; packaging; shipping; returns; inventory management.
- Complaints, faults, etc: what do you need to consider in case of issues arising?
- Growth: outline how you will handle items such as:
    - o Staffing?
    - o Not enough hours in the day?
    - o Sourcing funds?
- Don't forget to plan for things going wrong:
    - o What are the risks?
    - o How will you identify these?
    - o How will you mitigate these?

- Exit Strategy:
    o What are the plans to move away from the business?
    o What are the plans should things not work out the way you want them to?
    o How will you manage any debt generated by the business?
- Set yourself clear goals for the period that covers the time to setup your business and the first 3 months in operation.

I know I have said this already, but given its importance I will say it again: *The initial purpose of your business plan is to assist you in bringing your idea to life by identifying the key processes and steps that need to be completed prior to and post business launch.*

While you may have heard from other sources that your plan should forecast and plan ahead as far as 5 years, I personally think that to be unnecessary. It is hard enough to know what a new venture or even existing business will be doing in 12 months time, let alone 5 years. Yes, it's good to have long terms goals and ideas, and yes it's not a bad idea putting these into your business plan. But especially when you are just starting out there is no need to 'over vision' the process, rather, just try to get your head around what you need to do to get started with your business and what you need to do in your first 3 months of being in operation.

Once your business has been operational for 3 months revisit your plan and update the information so that the plan is now focusing on growth strategies rather than the initial startup strategies. Particularly focus on your financials, and with a few months of operational data now at your disposal you should be able to create financial sheets (e.g. budgets, forecasts) that are a bit more in line with the realities of your business (although you will find that in most cases a business needs at least one years of trading history to really be able to develop more accurate financial spreadsheets).

Once in place and the business is operational, I would recommend reviewing your business plan every 6 months:

1. First review and compare your business plan with where you actually got to in the past 6 months with your business. Did you hit all of your goals? If no what prevented you?
2. Second, modify your plan in light of your current situation.

3. Third, draw up new goals to achieve over the next 6 and 12 months.

Our next lesson will look at business structures.

Lessons on Business Structures

In Australia, before you can open your doors and trade you must register as a business with the relevant government authorities. This is a critical process that could see you with a lot of pain if done incorrectly. As such, I highly recommend you talk to an accountant and a business solicitor for advice on taxation and the options that exist around business structures prior to opening your doors as a business.

Getting the right structure from the beginning can allow for more flexibility in your business (for example making it easier to bring on stakeholders etc.), provides optimum taxation advantages, affects your operating costs, affects the way other businesses transact with you and can also give you better personal protection should the business turn sour.

Deciding on your business structure

A number of business structures exist in Australia that you can consider. The main ones include:

- Sole trader

- Partnership

- Trust

- Company

Sole Trader

This is the easiest, quickest and least expensive structure to set up. This structure gives you full control of your business, but also means that you are legally responsible for all aspects of the business. Should things go bad with the business you can quite easily lose your personal assets including any motor vehicles or property. From a taxation point of view, any business income you earn (after relevant expenses) is to be reported in your personal tax return. Thus, your sole trading business pays the same tax rate that an individual Australian Resident does. You are allowed to employ staff as a sole trader, keeping in mind that you will be responsible for paying their relevant taxes and superannuation contributions (don't forget to pay yours as well).

For simplicity purposes I have used a sole trading entity a number of times in my business career. For me, the main draw cards have been the ease of setup, the low cost of entry and the ease with which I could change structures as my business grew. The main negative has been the lack of support that I have received from other businesses, many of whom have either been very reluctant to deal with me or have outright refused to do business with me due to my sole trading business structure.

If you want to significantly grow your business then you may wish to consider one of the other options.

Partnership

Similar to the Sole Trading entity, a Partnership is easy and inexpensive to set up. Unlike a Sole Trader however you are not alone – you share the responsibility of managing the business and the income generated by the business with all your partners. Business assets are jointly owned by you and your partners. Any debts incurred are a liability of you and your partners, and as a result should the business run into trouble your personal assets could be lost. Any income that is generated is distributed amongst the partners (dependent on share of business) and the individual partners are responsible for their own tax payments. Be aware though that working in partnership with others can be tricky: there is plenty of potential for disputes and any liabilities that are incurred by other partners is the responsibility of every partner in the partnership.

Trusts

These are utilized when you wish to hold properties or income for the benefit of the beneficiaries of the Trust. Setting up and maintaining a trust is expensive and complex, however you do receive greater asset protection as an individual. Income generated by the Trust is distributed amongst the beneficiaries as determined by the trustee of the trust. The beneficiaries are then liable to pay tax on the amount they receive, based on their income tax rates for that year. Should any income remain undistributed, the Trust faces a very high tax rate on this amount.

Companies

Complex and more expensive to set up and operate than the other options mentioned above, this structure gives you the greatest personal protection. Regulated by the Australian Securities and Investments Commission (ASIC), the company structure enables you to add or take off shareholders with relative ease and gives you greater credibility with clients and other businesses. Companies are considered a separate legal entity, which means assets can be held in their own name. They can also sue and be sued. As a shareholder you are not liable for the debts generated by the business, however, as a director you may still be personally liable for any losses should the business run into trouble. The company pays tax on all profits generated by the business at a rate of 30% (which is current at the time of writing this book). Profits can be reinvested in the company or distributed amongst the shareholders. Companies also have the benefit of being easy to sell or pass on to other people or entities.

My experience

As mentioned at the beginning of this chapter, I recommend you involve your professional advisors when making decisions on business structures.

I started Goby as a sole trader, forming a company as business picked up. Within that company John and I were the two shareholders and also the two company directors.

SpindaCorp also started as a sole trading entity. This was for one main reason: so we could start trading ASAP. Once we spoke to our accountants and solicitors about our future plans, SpindaCorp was set up as a company. This time our respective trusts were the shareholders, with Stuart and I being the company directors.

This structure gave a better solution for us in regards to financial disbursements, and an additional layer of protection for personal assets. Please note: the corporate law sector is complex and forever changing. Advice that was valid one year ago may no longer be suitable today. It is important that you always seek independent advice from a reputable solicitor and accountant. One more thing: the old saying 'you get what you pay for' is very very true when it comes to such advice. Don't look for the cheapest professional that you find in your local newspaper. Instead, ask around and find someone that comes with plenty of positive feedback and don't hesitate to pay more for good advice.

We've so far touched on a number of important factors to consider prior to starting your business. There is just one more topic we need to discuss: Business Partners.

Lessons on Business Partners

For me this is a critical one as I have experienced firsthand the effect a poor business partnership can have on an organization. The decision to bring on a partner should not be taken lightly and should be better thought through than just having a beer at a pub and agreeing to work together.

A successful working partnership, like the one I had with John in Goby, can provide your business with a better rounded approach to decision making and can push your business forward at a much faster pace than if it was all up to you. There are certainly some great benefits to be gained from a partnership, but you must weigh this up with the flip side, which can lead to the collapse of your business.

If you asked me if I would take on a business partner again, my reply would be something along the lines of 'Yes I would, but only if the person coming on board brought with them an added value to the business without which the growth of the business is hindered or slowed down'.

When considering a business partner it is best to look for someone who can match your energy and work ethic, and bring with them skills and work capabilities that you are either lacking, do not enjoy (example: you hate talking to clients, so an ideal business partner could be one who is strong in this area), or have had exposure to but are not apt at. Depending on their level of involvement within your business you should also consider their leadership skills and how they would gel with any future employees.

There are several types of business partners. They can be:

- Purely financial and silent in the actual running of your business.
- Purely consultative, silent in the background but providing you with guidance, mentoring and coaching. If they are from within your industry they may also be used to open doors otherwise closed to you.
- Fully active and operational in all aspects of your business.
- A combination of all of the above.

Be Careful – Document Everything!

Should you decide that a partner is required, no matter what form they join you, I have one simple advice that you should not side step: **don't start any business partnership without appropriately documenting the** basis of the partnership, who will do what, the exact timeframes and expectations, exit strategies, plans for any issues/disputes that may arise and of course documenting any and all financial transactions.

In my own businesses I've had 3 types of partners:

- Silent financial
- Active nonfinancial
- Active financial

The only one that had any sort of documentation was the first one. The other two were handshake type agreements: I like you, you like me; you look like a nice person so let's do business together. Although this handshake approach worked with John (the active nonfinancial partner), such an arrangement was completely inappropriate with Stuart. In fact, when it came to the disputes with Stuart, in hindsight many months of financial bickering would have been avoided had I created appropriate agreements from the beginning. It was certainly a very painful way of learning such a simple lesson.

The relationship that forms as a result of a business partnership can be likened to that of a married couple, especially if your partner will be actively involved in the venture. Just like the success of a married couple is so closely linked to communication, so too is the success of your business partnership. It is thus absolutely critical for you and your business partner to regularly communicate with each other, to be honest, upfront, ethical and completely transparent with each other. Having said this, I strongly believe that it is foolish to think that it's possible to work with a business partner and never have disagreements. Being well prepared though from the beginning of the partnership can save you a lot of future problems and a lot of arguments that could potentially ruin your business.

As you read earlier, the lack of communication between Stuart and I made life difficult and led to many arguments in the later stage of business. These arguments revolved predominantly around:

1. Money

2. Debt

3. Staffing

4. Vision for the business

5. Inequality in the energy we each put into the partnership

Openness and honesty is especially crucial when money comes into the picture. Being at the crux of business, money is one of the key reasons for arguments and partnerships not working out. The main issues I have personally had with my partners and money were:

1. Disagreements as to how much we each put into the business over a period of time and who has been repaid what amount.

2. A discrepancy between the amount of time and energy each party puts into the business and who should get paid what amount.

3. Disagreement as to how money should be spent within a company, especially how profits should be dealt with.

Things wouldn't have escalated into heated discussions had we bothered to document everything from the beginning, and had we faced each other with our issues from the onset. It was too easy however to ignore problems and just pretend that things will get better. Unfortunately, this attitude of hiding from problems is all too prevalent in business relationships. In this case, the hardest thing to do is also the smartest: **face your problems and tackle them head on!**

Suggestions to give your business partnership a strong potential to survive include:

1. Select the right partner. Don't just work with someone because you like them as a friend or because they are a nice person. Take the time in selecting a partner who complements your skills and who can bring something you can't to the venture.

2. Document everything before your working business partnership begins. If there are too many disagreements or conflicts at this point perhaps you need to reconsider if they are the right person for the role.

3. Work out a strategy for conflict resolution should a disagreement come up that neither of you are willing to budge on. Consider who you would appoint as a mediator, and consider what each of you would accept as an exit strategy.

4. Work out your possible exit strategies. Discuss where you each want to take the business and what you would accept as an exit option out of the business. Perhaps you want to build a business to sell off in a few years. Perhaps you want to build and hold, or even build and buy out your partner/s at a later stage. It's important to understand where you each stand on this issue. There is nothing worse than wanting to go

down one path, only to find out your partner wants to do the exact opposite, potentially wasting valuable time in forward movement and potentially missing out on a great opportunity.

5. It is vital to keep accurate records of everything. In your meetings nominate one of you to be the minutes taker and make sure you both get copies of these notes. Any time one of you puts more money into the business or takes out more than the nominated salary amount, document the transaction including:

If money is put into business:

   i. State the amount and depositor.

   ii. Will interest be charged by the depositor, and if yes at what rate?

   iii. When will the amount be repaid?

   iv. How will it be repaid (e.g. monthly equal amounts, one lump sum when the business can afford it, etc).

   v. Will the depositor receive any other benefits by putting in more money (outside of interest on this) and if yes, what are these (e.g. they get x% higher profit share or work one day less per week)?

vi.   Both parties to sign and date and both to get a copy.

vii. Make sure you (or your bookkeeper) update your accounting ledger accordingly so it is accurately reflected in your figures.

If money is taken out of the business:

i.   State amount and to whom.

ii.   Will the business charge interest and if yes at what rate?

iii. How will this be repaid?

iv.   Both parties to sign, date and to get a copy.

v.   Make sure you or your bookkeeper updates your accounting ledger accordingly so it is accurately reflected in your figures. The decision is yours (and your business partners) regarding what minimum amount will be documented in this format; my suggestion would be to document all transactions which will save you a lot of arguments should things turn sour!

6. Communicate with each other. I mentioned this one just before, and cannot emphasize it enough. Talk about any issues as they come up, be honest about your feelings and learn to respect each other's differing views and

opinions. Above all, remember that conflict can have positive outcomes – it can improve processes, improve efficiencies, challenge the status quo and can create new initiatives that wouldn't have otherwise surfaced.

In reality you will find yourself spending more time with your business partner than with your life partner and family, so it's important you can work together harmoniously whilst respecting each other's views and opinions.

Lessons on Marketing

I often went fishing up in Maine during the summer. Personally, I am very fond of strawberries and cream, but I have found that for some strange reason, fish prefer worms. So when I went fishing, I didn't think about what I wanted. I thought about what they wanted. I didn't bait the hook with strawberries and cream. Rather, I dangled a worm or a grasshopper in front of the fish and said "Wouldn't you like to have that?" - Dale Carnegie

Marketing is a complex topic on its own, with some people studying years at university to work this one out. For me, marketing has always been a challenging task – one that requires you to carefully weigh up how your hard earned money will be spent such that you maximize its return to you. I have spent years trying different approaches and have spent literally hundreds of thousands of dollars on everything from online pay per click adverts to printed journal ads and printed fliers. There is a lot to marketing and although I will give you some basic information, I highly recommend you read up and further educate yourself on marketing techniques and strategies.

Before we get started on marketing itself, let's take a look at branding your business, as this will have a great impact on how you approach your marketing.

Branding

Part of the Oxford dictionary definition of a brand is:

<u>**noun**</u>

- A type of product manufactured by a particular company under a particular name: *a new brand of soap powder.*
- A brand name: *the firm will market computer software under its own brand; it takes a long time to build a brand.*
- A particular identity or image regarded as an asset: *you can still invent your own career, be your own brand.*
- A particular type or kind of something: *they entertained millions with their inimitable brand of comedy.*

In my simplistic view, the brand of a company represents the company's personality. The logo, business name, slogan (tagline), color scheme, value proposition and customer interaction all represent the foundations for a brand, and it is important that you get these elements right. Why? Because correct branding will allow you to connect with your target market and your potential customers, helping drive more business through your doors. Understanding your customers and the image that you want your customers to have of your business are important aspects of brand development, with a mismatch potentially affecting your bottom line.

As mentioned above, some of the different elements that form the foundations of a brand include:

1. **Business/Brand Name** – This is an obvious one. Without a business name you have no business! Try and select a name that is easy to remember, that is available preferably both as a .com and a .com.au url (domain name), that isn't infringing on other's trademarks and that is actually available to trademark for yourself. And of course, the name needs to be available for business name registration and if you are setting up a company then preferably it will be available as a company name too.

2. **Logo** – The logo can be as simple as the words and font used, or more complex with a combination of images and words being used. My tip here is to keep your logo simple. Look at the biggest brands in the world – the vast majority keep things simple when it comes to their logo. Why? Many reasons, including ease of recognition and remembrance, and the fact

that a simple logo is easier to use in various mediums without the risk of losing quality or 'decipherability'.

Check out the logos below as examples of what others businesses have done. Do you notice a pattern here? Look at the brands. Which are high end? Which are low end? And how have they positioned themselves brand wise as a result of the logo/colors/font chosen?

Note: the above logos are trademarks of the relevant companies and have been used for example purposes only.

3. **Slogan/tagline** – Can be used to either tell the customer what you do, or to relay a message that aligns with the 'personality' of the business. For example, Nike's™ 'Just Do It'™ slogan has nothing to do with its products, rather, it aligns with their brand attitude and personality of being sporty, active, uninhibited, youthful, cool. Digital Duet's slogan is 'Business Builders'. I opted for this as it's a simple, clean way of communicating what lies at the core purpose of the business.

4. **Color Scheme** – As with the logo and the rest of the brand imagery, you have a lot of variability and options here. Just bear in mind that less is better, and that irrespective of the colors chosen, your logo should also always look great in traditional black and white. One thing to bear in mind when considering color schemes is that traditionally brands that tend to be positioned at the 'cheaper' end of the market often tend to have the most colors in their logo, with brands at the high end often tending to be the simplest with a combination of just pure black and white.

5. **Font Style** – As per the logo and colors, the font you choose will have an impact on the whole look and feel of the brand and will help

communicate your brand 'personality' to the consumer.

6. **Value Proposition** – This brand attribute is often misunderstood, but in actual fact is simply this: it is the answer to the consumers question of 'why should I buy from you, or use your services?'. If we think of your business, the value proposition is a powerful statement that should be found on your marketing material and your website. A clever value proposition should make clear why customers need to come to you versus the competition, how your product solves a problem or generates improvements, and what benefits are delivered. Here are two of my favorite examples:

Skype: Wherever you are, wherever they are – Skype keeps you together.

Salesforce: No hardware. No software. No boundaries.

7. **Customer Interaction** – Often times business owners I meet have all of the above branding elements in place, only to be let down by the experience their customer has with the business. The element of customer interaction is a mission

critical one – you can have the most awesome branding with the best looking website and marketing material and funky office spaces where you hold weekly cocktail parties, but all of that is pointless if your customer has a poor experience with your business time and time again. So, to become a well rounded strong brand with a loyal following, it is imperative that you setup a culture built around the customer experience – one which every single member of your team follows and lives by. Do this, and you will not only become a brand you customers love, but you will also become a workplace of choice, where your employees enjoy coming to each workday and where they bring their 'A' game at all times.

As you can see, a brand is more than one single element. It is a combination of various elements coming together to form the overall perception you want the market place to have of your business. As previously mentioned, your brand will help you differentiate your business in the market place and has the potential to help drive the growth of the business, provided it becomes a brand of choice for your customers.

Now, building a reputable brand takes time, years in fact, but regardless of the time, it should really begin with an understanding of your target market. When creating the various elements that will represent your business brand, regularly turn to this knowledge of your market sector.

Let's look at a couple of my businesses and how I approached branding them.

SpindaCorp – Medical Recruitment Company

Business Name: Said what the company did in a short, easy to spell word.

Logo: Doctors' stethoscope in front of the words, highlighting the health focus of the business. The words were bold, identifying with the serious nature of the business.

Color Scheme: Subtle, down to earth colors that indicated that this is a professional organization.

Font: Strong and bold - representing seriousness, professionalism.

Slogan: Recruiting the best Medical minds for Australia.

Goby – Online textbook retailer

Business Name: Short and snappy name that fits the online market by being easy to remember and spell. Name has nothing to do with the services of the business, thus doesn't lock the business into a specific sector.

Logo: Capital G in the shape of Australia, indicating that it's an Australian business. Logo looks young, funky and fun, attracting the student market.

Color Scheme: The bright blue color symbolizes a blue ocean or blue sky – indicating towards endless potential.

Font: Word 'Goby' written in a relatively fun font that indicates to the market that the business doesn't take itself all too seriously.

Slogan: For students, by students. This clearly tells the market who this business is aimed at.

I could have just as easily created a fun, laid back brand for SpindaCorp; and a serious professional one for Goby. This image however was not how I wanted to position either of the businesses, nor was it how the market would have expected to see the brands. It takes a bit of experimentation to come up with a combination that works for your business and that portrays the message you want to communicate.

Creating your brand is an important step so don't rush it. Remember that once you get your business setup and you have business cards, stationery, websites, and possible office signage containing your branding, it will be much harder to do anything should you decide to change your mind about the font you used for example or you realize you branded the wrong way!

Some of my branding tips:

1. Understand your market sector – Who are your customers? What are their expectations?

2. Know how you want to be perceived by your customers.

3. Choose your branding components in such a way that together, and individually, they represent how you want your customers to perceive you.

4. Branding goes beyond the logo and color scheme. The way you and your team interact with customers and the experiences your customers have with your business will all add to the overall brand image. As such, always be

aware of how your business interacts with customers and ensure that your products/services deliver on all promises made.

5. It is difficult and time intensive to build a strong, reliable brand that customers automatically turn to and trust. It is very easy however to ruin a brand and thereby your business reputation. **Never forget this.**

Marketing

The goal of any marketing campaign is to:

1. Increase your brand awareness in the marketplace.

2. Tell your market what your business offerings are.

3. Generate customer enquiries.

Unfortunately there isn't a one shoe fits all marketing approach for all industries. I often get asked by clients to give them a 'magic marketing bullet', but the truth is this doesn't exist. Our society is incredibly diverse, so trying to approach every industry with the same method will not work. Throughout my business career I've had to vary and evolve marketing techniques as my target customers and products changed. Even within the same business I've constantly had to fine tune and vary my strategies, and even to this day after years of experience I sometimes find myself experimenting with various approaches to find a suitable and viable marketing solution.

The one key lesson I have taken away from years of experimentation is simple but incredibly powerful: **the greater your understanding of your target market, the greater your results will be**.

It is because of this that EVERY marketing strategy should start with an analysis of who the key target customers are.

Let's take a look at a couple of real life examples of mine, mapping out the key target customers within the businesses so you can see how this works in real life. Please turn to the next page.

Business: Goby

Target Market: University Students

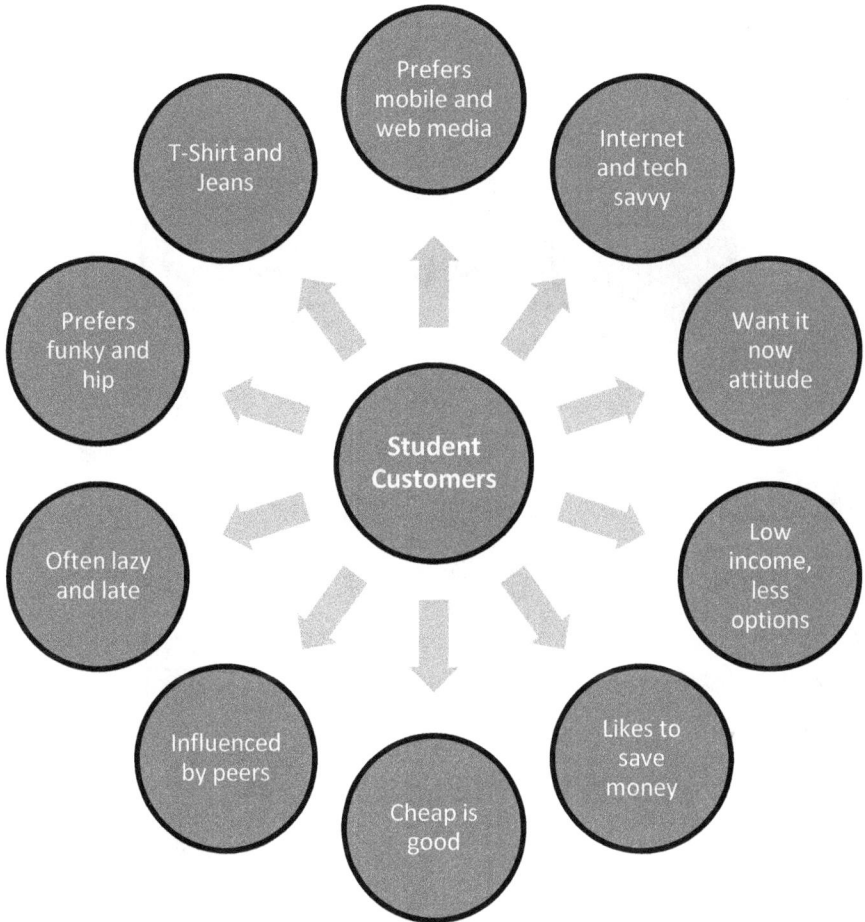

Business: SpindaCorp

Target Market: Doctors

Sub Market: Specialist Doctors

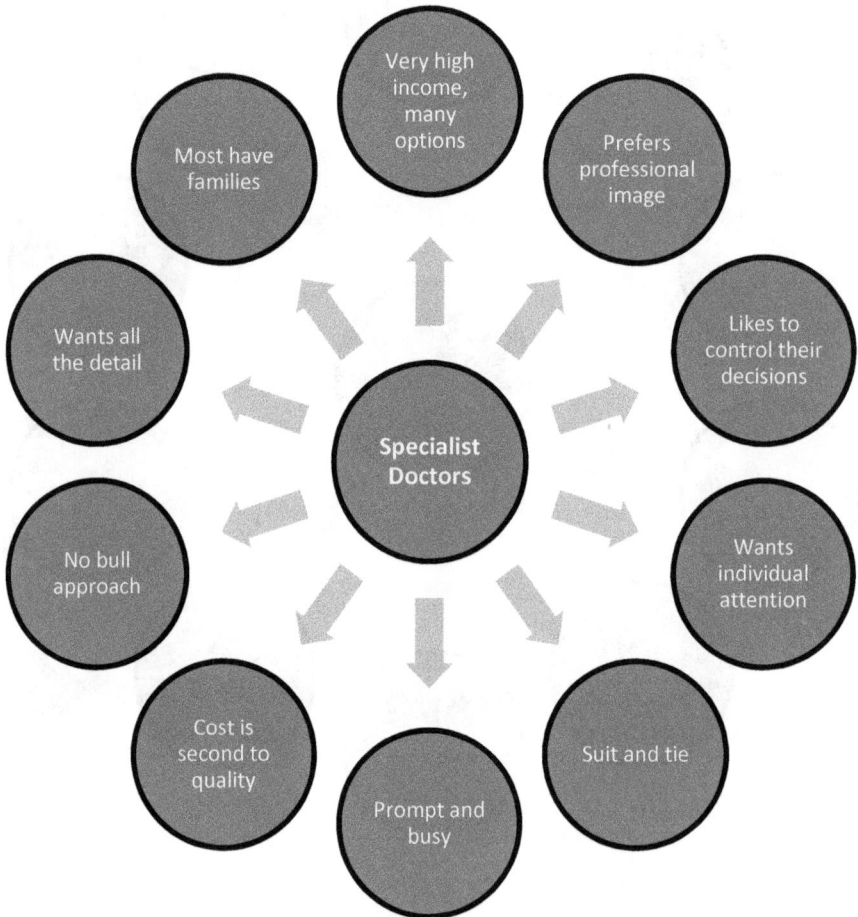

As a starting point in creating your own marketing campaign, a target customer map like the ones we just had a look at will help you clearly identify with your target market and get a clearer picture of who you are targeting with your marketing efforts.

From here, the next step in the development of your marketing strategy is to understand what options you have in terms of actual marketing tools by creating what I call a Marketing Medium Map.

Referring to your target customer map, the creation of a marketing medium map will give you a clear picture of all the options available to you in terms of communicating with, and to the target customer. The following pages demonstrate three examples of medium maps that I used in my businesses.

GOBY - Students

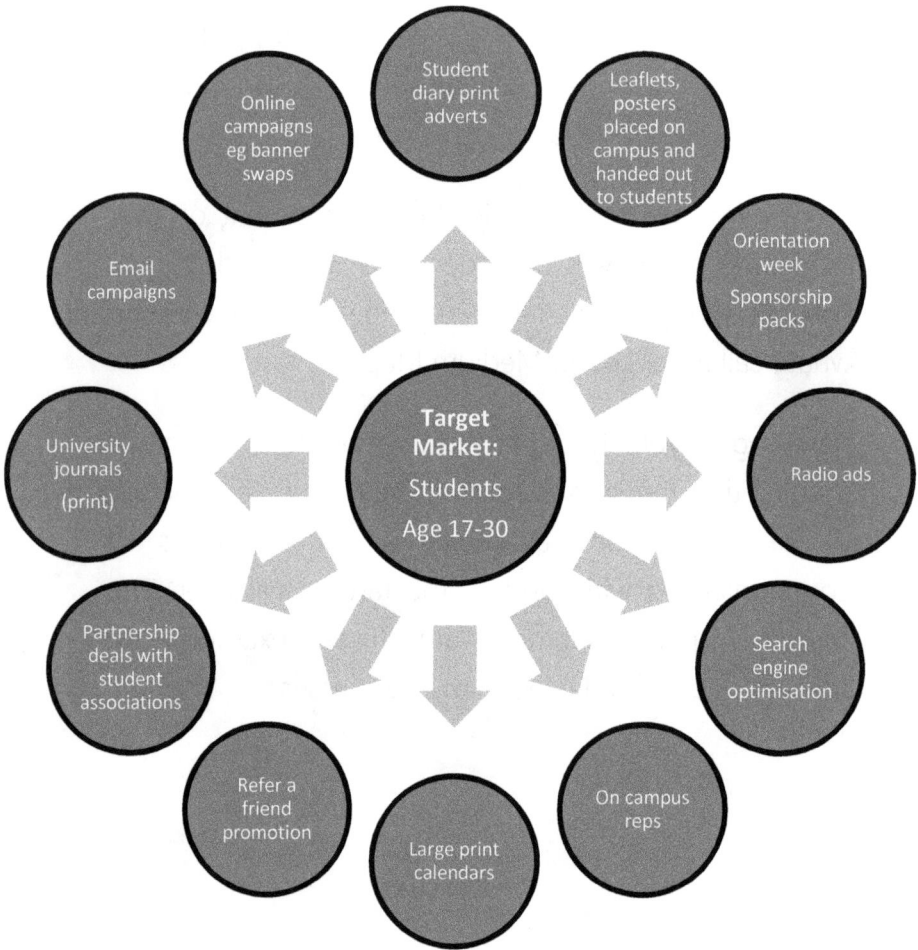

SpindaCorp - Doctors

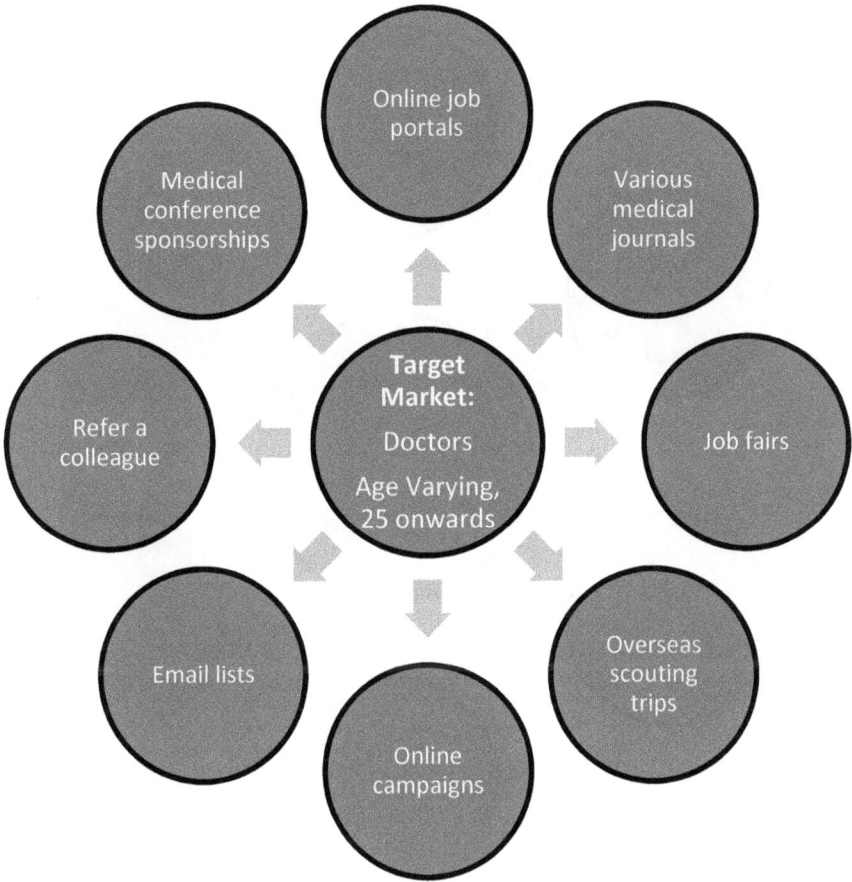

SpindaCorp – Clients

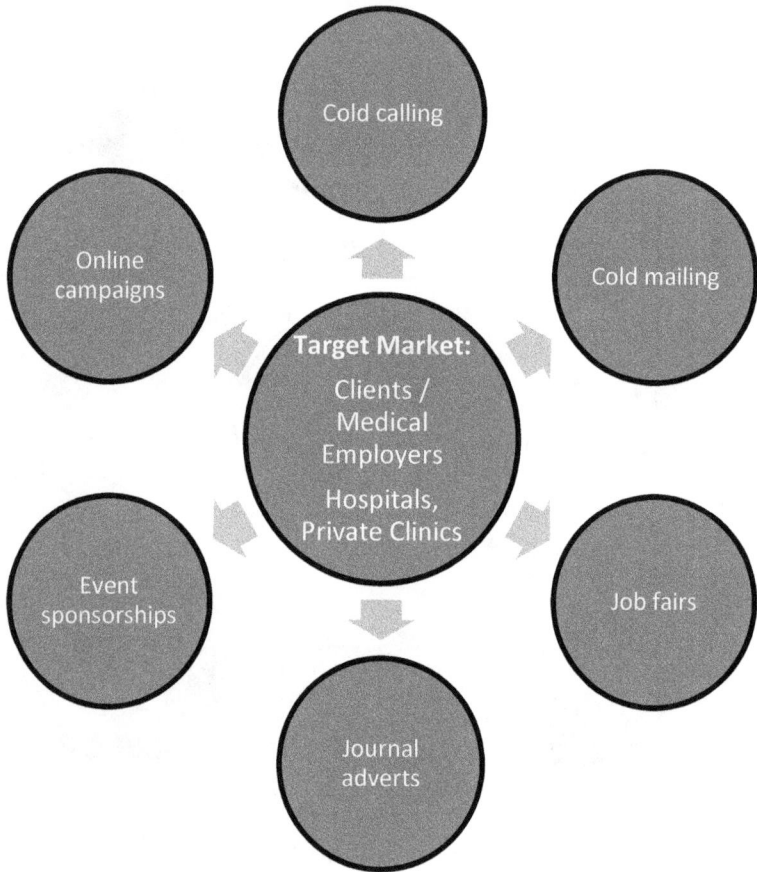

Diagram with central circle labelled "Target Market: Clients / Medical Employers — Hospitals, Private Clinics" surrounded by circles: Cold calling, Cold mailing, Job fairs, Journal adverts, Event sponsorships, Online campaigns.

Now it's your turn! Grab a piece of paper and sketch it all out. List everything you can think of. Be creative. Be outlandish! That's how great marketing ideas often come about!

After you have created your marketing medium map, it's time to put on the research hat and answer the following for each of your listed options:

- Timeframe to produce advert.

- Cost to produce advert.

- Time to get advertising material to the market.

- Cost to get advertising material to market.

The easiest way to do this is by putting it all into a marketing medium table. Have a look at my simple example below:

Option	Timeframe	Cost	Time to get to market	Cost to get to market
Large print calendars (10,000 pieces)	One day to design poster; One week for printing; One week for dispatch.	~$8,000	2-4 weeks from receipt of posters.	$650 to distribute around the country.

Fliers to hand out on campus (100 pieces)	Couple of hours to design and print yourself.	$13	Couple of hours placing fliers around the University Campus.	Free if doing yourself.
Google Ad Words™	Hour or two to create several ads.	Free to setup.	Instant.	$5 max limit per day; $150 per month.
University journal monthly print ad	One week to design and proof advert.	Varying $500 - $3,000 per advert, depending on size.	Once per month - printed version.	Included in print cost.
Partnership deals with student associations	Several months.	Usually they will get a % kickback per referral.	Several months.	Nil.
Radio adverts	One month to prepare advert.	$1,000 - $3,000 to create advert, followed by $750 per airplay of the advert.	Air time can start as soon as advert is complete.	$750 per airplay of the advert.
Banner swapping with partner websites	One week to arrange deals and to create banners.	Free.	Exposure starts as soon as swap negotiated and banners designed.	Free.

Once you have created this table for yourself it's time to work out how much money you have available to spend on marketing activities. My first ever marketing campaign at the start of Get Healthy had a total budget of $20! This was enough to get some fliers printed and pasted all over the campus.

As sales grew and the business started making money, I could afford to put aside $500 for a bigger marketing campaign. This time around I ran a BBQ which gave me free exposure in the health faculty newsletter plus I continued posting fliers all over the campus and getting up before lectures to talk about my business services. I then mirrored this strategy at another university. The total cost of all of this came in under my budget. I could have easily spent the $500 elsewhere, such as placing one single advert in the University journal, but one advert wouldn't have given me the diverse exposure that I was after.

Fast forward in time, with the growth in the business I could afford to allocate $15,000 towards the marketing of the new Goby website. This amount gave me a lot of options, but I knew that I had to be careful to not waste this money on futile attempts. Again I created a marketing medium table similar to the one above, and came up with a strategy that included a combination of posters, fliers, print magazine adverts, BBQ's, partnerships with other businesses and online adverts. The biggest dilemma I had was tossing up between posters or radio adverts. In the end I decided to go with posters as they could give me exposure all year round, provided that the students placed them on their walls and referred to them.

In addition to the paid marketing, I contacted a number of newspapers to see if they were interested in running a free story on us. I didn't think anything would come of this, but to my amazement The Australian, a large national newspaper, called me back asking for an interview! The interview took place only a week or so after the initial call was made, and before we knew it a nice full color article appeared in this national newspaper just as we were pushing forward with the rest of our campaign.

I tackled marketing SpindaCorp in the exact same way. I first analyzed my target market, then created a marketing medium map with a detailed table outlining all available mediums, pricing and timeframes. My first budget was $2,000 – at the launch of SpindaCorp. I had several available options, including spending the lot on two full page glossy color magazine adverts. Wanting a more widespread approach that incorporated multiple media, I opted for a campaign that included:

- Company service brochures delivered to prospective clients nationwide.

- A couple of small black and white adverts in a medical journal.

- Placing up multiple job adverts on two different online job boards.

- Setting up a number of Google AdWords campaigns.

I spread this out over three months and by the time I ran out of the allocated $2,000 I had generated enough revenue to continue marketing on a number of job boards. As the business grew, so too did my marketing budget, giving us greater reach and a wider range of mediums to tap into.

So now for one of those *'Million dollar questions'*.........

How much should you spend on marketing?????

This is a very commonly asked question to which I often reply with another question: 'How much can you afford to lose?'. As mentioned before there are no guarantees in marketing, so whatever you invest you have to be willing to take a hit on should your marketing activities flop (especially in a fresh business). If you are an existing business with at least a year behind you, then things are made easier in that you have historical data to use in forecasting future returns, and using historical marketing data to know what should work and what most likely won't. Even so, marketing should always be completed with a clear plan in place in order to give you the best chance for success.

Here are some handy marketing tips that I've picked up over the years:

1. Don't risk putting all your money into one single advert, especially if this is your first marketing campaign (example of this is investing everything into one single full page ad). You are better off running multiple smaller ad campaigns where your advert appears regularly over a period of time. Doing so will help maximize the number of potential customers seeing your brand (e.g. run ¼ page adverts in a trade journal over several consecutive issues rather than spending up on one single full page ad).

2. Increase your potential exposure by using a variety of media. I had great success with my Goby campaign which used a combination of offline media (posters, campus reps, a couple adverts in the university magazines, freebies with purchases) and online media (email campaigns,

banner adverts on partner sites and Google AdWords).

3. When looking at what available media you have to work with, try and think laterally. People tend to respond better to quirky, unusual, clever marketing as opposed to the traditional that they are used to. For example, sending free condoms with every student order during the Goby days significantly helped raise our brand awareness as students found the idea amusing and told their peers about it.

4. Marketing does not have to cost a fortune. There are a lot of free or cheap ways to get your name out to the public including writing informative blogs, running informative seminar nights, banner swaps with other business websites, joining local community groups, jumping on the social media wagon (more on this shortly) and many more that I am sure you will uncover.

5. Do your own research and have a look at how some of the biggest brands in the world advertise and market themselves. If we take a brand such as Coca Cola™ for example, you will notice that they are constantly pushing their

brand in a variety of media, using regularly updated adverts and styles that really appeal to their target market. Although chances are you won't even have 1/1,000th of their annual marketing budget at your disposal, you can still emulate their strategies to some degree in your own campaigns.

6. You should always be pedantic in the creation of any adverts or marketing material. People are judgmental, and the way you portray your business in your marketing material will affect sales. If you are not apt at using graphics programs or perhaps haven't got the best ad writing skills, seek out a friend to help you for free or go to an agency for assistance. This is definitely money well spent. And make sure that before you make anything public you have had input from friends and family on the look and feel of that material – it may look good to you, but others may just spot a mistake that you missed (this has happened to me on more than a few occasions...).

7. Know your target audience so you know how your ads and material should appear to them. In my case, adverts for Goby that targeted university students looked and read completely

different to those that were aimed at senior doctors with SpindaCorp. The first group wanted discounts and wanted to know we were cheap. The second group consisted of very high earning, serious individuals who demanded perfection, quality and a prompt service; here, substance and quality. Mismatch your campaign with your audience and expect poor results.

8. I have left the most important tip for last. Always provide exceptional service, follow through with promises made to customers and go beyond expectations. This advice is crucial to the overall success of your business. I mentioned earlier in the book that providing poor service after a successful initial marketing campaign with Goby significantly impacted the business in a very negative way. But don't just take my word for it: think back to times when a business did wrong by you. Did that affect the way you thought of them and did you tell anyone about your bad experience? On the flipside, have you ever had such good service that you think of that business first when requiring such services or products, even putting price as a second to their trustworthiness? Be a good business your

customers love dealing with and your marketing headaches may even disappear!

Marketing and Social Media

Social media has really taken the world by storm. Websites such as Facebook, LinkedIn and Twitter have made connecting with anyone, anywhere in the world a simple, effective process. With a large portion of the world's population hooked on social media, the doors are wide open for businesses to tap into new customers and reaffirm the loyalty of existing customers.

Nonexistent during my Goby days, social media only really became a tool in my marketing arsenal towards the end of the life of SpindaCorp. Now, several years post SpindaCorp, social media has grown to become a must have marketing tool for most businesses.

There are many benefits to using social media as part of your marketing strategy. Some of these include:

- Cost effective way of advertising to your audience.

- Simple to set up.

- Excellent way to engage with existing and potential customers.

- Great way of spreading the word about your business, including building your brand in the market place.

- Potential to open up new markets and help you reach customers who might previously have gone elsewhere.

- Excellent way to do market research and take customer feedback.

Keep in mind the following about social media for business: **having a presence on all of the social media outlets doesn't necessarily mean that you will generate extra sales, however, not being on social media can negatively affect your search engine rankings which can result in a lot of lost opportunities.**

A presence however is simply not enough anymore. In order to make the most of this platform for your business, you have to become an active member of the social community. So what does this mean?

Being active on social media means:

- Regularly releasing new posts and using this to start conversations with your audience.

- Interacting with your members by posting questions and comments that elicit a discussion, and that give you direct feedback.

- Promoting your social media pages on your website and on your offline marketing material.

- Asking your customers to follow you on the various social media websites.

- Asking satisfied customers to post positive comments onto your social media pages, and even onto their own.

- Tying in promotional marketing activities with social media - such as a special deal that is available only to those who follow your business social media pages (for example on Facebook those members who 'like' your page get special discounts).

- Evolving your sales process to include a social media sharing element (example: share this purchase right now for an immediate $10 discount off your current purchase).

- Don't forget: while social media can positively promote a business, it can also do the opposite very well. Stuff up and the whole online community will hear about it. So, if you don't want a tirade of negative comments and bad publicity, be sure to always look after your customers.

It's important to note that managing your social media accounts can take up a fair amount of your time, but there are tools available, such as Hoot Suite (www.hootsuite.com) which can make the management process so much easier.

Now, if you are wondering just how much time should be spent on social media per week, the answer really isn't black and white. It all depends on your industry, what role social media plays in your marketing, and of course how much time you can set aside to it. In my current business, I spend up to an hour each day on social media activities for business, however most days I only need to spend about 15minutes, and sometimes I may even have a week go by without a single post due to my schedule. So just work with what you have resource wise, perhaps even utilizing an employee or outsourcing to an agency if it becomes too much of a headache for you to personally handle.

Our next topic, Sales and Customer Relationship Management, goes hand in hand with Marketing.

Lessons on Sales and Customer Relationship Management

If marketing is the tool that lets your customers know you exist, then:

- sales is the tool that helps convert the potential customer who came through your marketing funnel into a real active customer who spends money with your business, and,
- customer relationship management (CRM) is the tool that helps you hedge against competition, increase repeat business and increase referred business.

These three tools go hand in hand if you want to successfully grow your business.

Although most people have a dislike for 'sales people' and dislike the term 'sales', the truth is that no business can exist without sales coming into the equation. This is especially true for young businesses as they try and establish themselves in the marketplace by convincing clients that theirs is the business they should be dealing with.

Love it or loathe it, sales is an unavoidable necessity EVERY business owner has to embrace and take part in.

If you want your business to grow and prosper you will want to learn how to secure new business whilst strengthening your existing relationships. Let's first look at sourcing and closing new business (sales), then let's see how to nurture that new business into a loyal repeat customer who refers you more new customers (this is what I call Customer Relationship Management, or CRM).

Sales

Sales is the key to turning potential customers into active ones. Whilst marketing is a great tool to tell the world you exist, it won't necessarily result in cash in the bank. Or if it does, it is often not at the levels that you need it to be to grow your business. I've seen many business owners spend a great deal of time and money creating marketing campaigns, only to have it all flop when it comes time to convert interested prospects into closed transactions where money has been exchanged. Many business owners sit back, waiting for their marketing campaign to draw in customers, expecting every enquiry to generate money. Unfortunately for them, although enquiries may be there, if the sales process is not followed through correctly then a lot of enquirers will take their money elsewhere. At best they get some sales, but it's in dribs and drabs, often barely enough to justify being in business.

If you truly want to get your business pumping then you must be prepared to step up and actively engage with your marketplace. So what does this mean? For me in Goby it meant getting up in front of dozens and even hundreds of students to talk about my business; in SpindaCorp it meant cold call after cold call to source clients and attend face to face meetings with potential candidates. In my current ventures I actively pursue new customer opportunities, and have built my business up without having to invest much money into the business as a result of the combined marketing and sales strategy I have in place.

At its simplest, sales means picking up the phone and cold calling potential clients, or pounding the pavement and visiting prospects door to door. I know this may sound daunting to you, but the reality is that if you don't get actively involved in selling your products or services to your market place, then how can you expect your business to become a success?

If the thought of talking to strangers about your business excites you then great, get to it!

If however you are breaking out in sweat just thinking about the idea of having to sell to someone, then let's have a look at some tips to help you get over that barrier.

First of all, can you answer this question: **Why does it scare you to approach strangers and talk to them about your business?**

From experience the answer to this will most likely be due to one or both of two main reasons:

1. Fear of rejection.

2. Lack of self confidence.

The fear of rejection would have to be the number one reason why many people in sales roles are only ever going to be average sales people. In response to possible rejection many people simply avoid the activities or encounters that could expose them to rejection. This sort of behavior in business however is counterproductive and irrational. Think about it: What's the worst thing that can happen if you cold call or approach a potential new client with your business services or products? As long as you were professional, courteous, polite and non-threatening in your tone and use of language, your worst outcome will be a client saying no thanks. The reality is that there is nothing wrong with someone saying no to your services, just as long as you move on and keep hunting for people who wish to say yes! In fact, you may find yourself getting a heck of a lot more 'no' responses than 'yes' responses, but you know what, that's fine! Why? Because success in sales can be linked to the law of averages – the more people you talk to, the greater your chance of achieving the numbers of 'yes' responses you were after. So, the more 'no's' you get, the greater the chances that you will also receive more 'yesses' as well!

Now, if you have no issues with someone saying no to you, but you lack the confidence to talk to strangers about your business, then I want you to look through all of the information which were used to make the decision to start your business in the first place.

Let's look at things logically. After going through all the steps of identifying, analyzing and strategically planning out your business idea, you should be confident in saying that you have the makings for a good business. If you are a product oriented business, then you would by now have a product or products that you believe in and are confident in. Similarly, if you are a service oriented business then you are confident in your services and know you can look after the needs of your clients.

So, if you are confident that you have a well researched business idea built on sound information, you have good products or services that you know you can deliver, then why would you have any hesitation to tell

the world how great your business really is???!!! And if you are hesitant about your products or services then maybe you need to revisit your idea and analyze it all over again.

If you don't have confidence in your business, neither will your customers!

If on the other hand you are happy with your business and know it's a good idea but you still lack confidence to talk to strangers, then I have one simple piece of advice for you: face your fears and don't let them hold you back.

Put in other words: *Suck it up princess and get to it!* Harsh? Maybe. Is it the truth? Yep!

You will find that as you start approaching people and the 'yesses' start rolling in you will quickly forget fear, replacing it with excitement as your success grows and grows.

The art of sales

Just as many successful businesses are built on ideas that provide a solution to a problem, success in sales is also built on finding a problem to which you have the solution. As simple as it sounds, if you want to success out of your sales activities simply identify a problem your potential customer has, to which your product or service is the solution. Be the solution and you will see results coming your way.

My first job out of school was a commission only, door to door sales role selling phone plans to business customers. It was my first exposure to sales, and hence I found the initial few weeks very challenging on a number of levels. Up until then I was always a quiet, shy introvert who shook at the thought of having to get up in front of a crowd or talk to complete strangers. It was because of this that I decided to take on such an uncomfortable job – I knew I needed to face my fears head on. Those first weeks were horrible. I had to force myself to walk into strange businesses and it took a lot of self pressure to utter my poorly prepared sales pitch. Needless to say, my income was dismal. A number of weeks into it I started getting the hang of the pitch and my sales slowly started increasing. I went from earning $90 in my first week to about $300 by the end of my 4th week. With practice my confidence grew stronger and as a result I cracked $500 in my 8th week. It was in this 8th week that I discovered a better way to pitch the products: target problems people were having with their current phone provider and show them solutions with my products. Up until then I would simply hurl myself into my usual sales pitch, taking hardly any time to breathe! After this realization however I focused in on their business and spent a bit more time understanding some of their issues with their existing phone company. Only after getting them to talk about their issues would I present my products, wrapped in an outer layer as a solution to their problems. This strategy worked wonders and my sales regularly hit $600 per week after this discovery.

Since then I have successfully used this technique (which is called solution selling) in all my business ventures and jobs working for others. I have of course made plenty of blunders and picked up many other good sales tips along the way from observation, education and experience.

Cold Calling Tips

1.	Before you pick up the phone, practice your spiel a few times. As you start dialing sit up straight and put a smile on your face. I've found this routine helps put me into the right mindset and prepares my confidence for the upcoming calls. And yeah I know, it sounds stupid for me to say 'put a smile on your face', but trust me, this simple act can have dramatic consequences in your attitude towards the call and hence the outcome of the call.

2. Always do your allocated lot of cold calling in the one sitting. Block off your schedule and don't stop until you have made all of your calls. Don't take other calls and don't check your email during this time.

3. Always be courteous, polite and professional. Never be pushy or aggressive as that sort of attitude will get you nowhere.

4. Always ask for permission to talk before launching into your spiel. E.g. 'Good afternoon Mr. Smith. My name is Peter Spinda and I am the Director of SpindaCorp medical recruitment agency. May I have a moment of your time please?' If you get a yes, fantastic – thank them and keep talking through your spiel. If you get a no, ask what the most suitable time to call on them would be. Now I know there are many other ways you could start off a cold call pitch, so what I am telling you here is what I have found to work best for me and my personality.

5. Be prepared for rude people, for rejection and being hung up on! Don't let this get to you – keep smiling, stay positive and never forget tip #3.

Sales Meeting Tips

1. This one is for the guys out there: Guys, before you hit the pavement go and look in the mirror! Do you look like you've just crawled out of bed? This is an important rule – always look professional when dealing with clients. This means your hair is combed/styled, your breath is fresh and you are either shaved or have neatly trimmed facial hair. Get rid of any facial piercings and put on some deodorant. Basic hygiene stuff, but you would be amazed how many guys miss this! And yeah I know, the hippie look is the 'in' thing, and it may actually suit you well and you could get away with the look, but if you really want to be taken seriously then you need to act and look serious. Just my advice. Take it or leave it...

2. Listen when your customer is talking. Take in what they are saying and talk to your customers about the services/products that they are interested in, not just the ones you want to push.

3. Communicate honestly with your customers. Don't tell fibs or make up nonexistent product or service features just to make a sale! If your product or service is not right for them then tell them and recommend someone else – this is an incredibly powerful technique that will give you a lot of credibility and referred business.

4. Don't be afraid to ask for your clients business. The age old saying of 'if you don't ask, you don't get' is very true for sales! This is one of the most important steps in closing a sale and is the one most often missed by average sales people – hence why they are only average.

5. Keep away from closed questions, unless you specifically want a closed answer. Closed questions include: Do you like what I have shown you? An open question version of this would be: What do you like about what I have shown you so far?

6. Refer back to tips #3 and #5 from cold calling.

Closing the Sale

1. As I said earlier, average sales people are poor closers. You can have a great time in your client meetings, you may have just given the sales

pitch of your life, but if you stuff up your close then chances are your client will say 'thank you for your time, we'll get back to you'....and of course they never get back to you and for some reason they won't return your emails or calls...weird seeing as you nailed the pitch hey?

2. So following on from the above point, never assume you have the sale until the deal is done, the paperwork is signed and the ink has dried! I have on far too many occasions counted my money (and spent the money), even before having the deal fully closed, only to get a rude shock when the client goes to another provider. Put simply: Assumptions can be dangerous.

3. Closing simply means asking for your clients business. Once you have gone through your sales pitch and you have answered any questions your client may have, you are ready to ask that all important question: 'How many widgets would you like to purchase?"

4. Is the prospect still not buying after a closing attempt? Then maybe you need to retrace your steps, make sure you asked the relevant questions and re-state the key points of your sales pitch. Often times decisions aren't made

because the prospect is still not 100% sure about your product or service, and they need that extra reassurance before they commit.

5. Sometimes, try as you may, you won't close a prospect. No worries there, be courteous, and leave on a positive note. Follow them up with an email and phone call within a week of the meeting, sometimes people just need time to digest information. And after this, add them to your database and keep regularly marketing to them.

After the Sales Meeting

1. If possible or appropriate to your circumstances, follow up your sales call within 24 hours with an email thanking them for their time to meet with you. If there were things you promised to follow up on then do so as soon as you can, always keeping your client informed if there is going to be a delay in getting promised information to them.

2. Deliver on everything you promise during your sales meeting.

Getting good at sales for most people means they need to do a lot of practice at making sales. Besides actual practice, I would also recommend you read books on the topic and attend sales courses run by professional instructors.

Customer Relationship Management

You have done a lot of hard work in getting customers to turn to your business. What you do next is even more important than closing the sale. Building a successful business that will last the years requires more than one off sales and a continuous reliance on new business. It requires dedicated repeat customers who not only use your services, but also refer business to you. Looking after your customers should be your number one priority at the front end of your business, and this is what Customer Relationship Management is all about.

Learning how to build strong relationships and how to leverage off of your trusted existing clients has the following benefits:

- Provides your business with regular repeat business.

- Greater rate of referrals from established customers – thus the more referrals, the less time and money you need to spend on sourcing new customers and the more time you have to focus on existing customers.

- Hedges against competition – clients who trust and know you are less likely to be swayed by new or even existing competitors.

- Hedges against possible loss of a client – if you have a good client base, losing one or two won't have as dramatic an effect on your business as it otherwise would.

- Higher chance that your invoices will be paid on time, every time, and if for some reason your client runs into financial trouble they are more likely to be honest with you about their situation.

Building Client Relationships

At its heart, CRM is about providing exceptional service to your clients every time. It is about becoming their trusted advisor, someone who knows and understands their business, whom they can turn to for solutions and advice. Irrespective of what industry you are in and whether you are selling a product or a service, the strategy behind building successful business relationships is the same.

As pointed out in the sales section, your first encounter with a new client should leave them feeling like they have been treated by a professional who wants to help them and who is not focused on making a quick buck. It is imperative that at this point, whatever you promise to do or follow up on occurs in a timely manner, and whatever you promise your product/s to do that they can actually do without any problems.

Beyond all the niceties, things that have successfully worked for me in building very strong client relationships include:

- Setting myself apart from the pack

Don't follow what everyone else is doing in your industry; step out and be different! Shortly after starting SpindaCorp it became abundantly clear to me that very few other medical recruiters took the time to really communicate with and get to know clients or candidates. So, to set myself apart from the pack I went the extra mile with my clients: I took a week out and drove about 3,000km's to personally meet with my most important contacts on the Eastern seaboard of Australia. As business grew, I swapped driving the long distances opting instead to fly, and I made it my business to travel every couple of months to catch up with my clients face to face. On more than one occasion I flew from Brisbane to Sydney (about a 2,000km round trip) just to have a one hour coffee with an important client, leaving in the morning, getting back home that afternoon.

I extended this personalized service to my candidates as well. Each time a candidate came in from overseas to view job sites I would take them and their new employer out to a very nice dinner. It sounds crazy, but I would fly to wherever they were coming to within Australia just for dinner. I cannot stress however the importance this level of relationship management had on growing SpindaCorp so quickly. As a testament, to this day, years after having walked away from SpindaCorp I can call up my previous clients and have great friendly conversations with them, with some of them and many candidates becoming friends of mine.

- Communication

It is all too easy in today's modern world to send someone an email and forget about communicating via the phone or meeting face to face. This however is a potentially costly mistake, as emails do not allow you to build quality rapport with your clients. While I utilize emails very frequently for business, I ensure that I take the time and call my clients regularly. This is especially so when I need to discuss an important matter or need urgent clarification over something. Putting email and phone aside, I cannot stress this statement enough: face to face meetings are an important communication tool to solidify your relationships and should always be part of your CRM process.

- Service

Selling to a customer and making promises is one thing. Actually delivering and following up on this is another. Any promises made must be followed up on within 24 hours at latest. If there are delays I would advise the client as soon as the delay is apparent, and keep them regularly updated as to when their request will be completed. When I was selling ties on eBay I set myself a goal to get my products to the customers as quickly as possible. Knowing that Australia Post provides a next day service to many regions of Australia if posted before 6pm the day before, I would do everything possible to have same day orders that have been paid for, posted on the same day. Many of my customers were surprised the next day when their order turned up at their door and as a result I received referred business and great positive feedback.

With SpindaCorp, I would make it a habit to send emails to clients and candidates at all hours of the day. Sometimes I would compose emails late afternoon and hold off sending them until I got to bed at midnight. This way, the next morning my email was the first they would see, and would also indicate to them the long hours I dedicated to the business. I would also set myself a response target to emails and would do my best to reply to all emails within a matter of hours of receipt. I monitored this each week, with the aim of continual improvement.

- Honesty

This is one that can catch out even the smoothest of operators! It is all too easy in the heat of a sale or excited conversation to make promises about your business that are simply not true or you cannot possibly deliver on. To save yourself embarrassment and the loss of a client be honest about the capabilities of the products and/or the services you offer. And if you realize that your business cannot meet the client's request, tell them and recommend a business that can. All too often business owners are scared of referring to other businesses, thinking it will kill theirs. What they don't realize is that this act will most likely have the opposite effect – you will become know as a reliable and honest operator who runs a business that clients can trust. I have turned business away on a number of occasions now, and on almost every occasion the client referred me more business, and the business I referred to reciprocated the gesture. It turned out to be win win for all.

In short, CRM can be summed up in these words: **look after your customers and they will look after you.**

Lessons on the Growing Business

There once was a man who lived in a small village and he enjoyed a little fishing. In fact his fishing was successful enough to support his family, which only took about 3 or 4 days per week of work. When his work was done he would enjoy the afternoon with his family. A meal together, a siesta, and then play his guitar, sing songs, share laughter with his family, and he knew he would spend the remainder of the evening in the company of his loving wife.

It so happened that one day as he returned from his fishing venture and took his catch to the market place, a business man took notice of the skilled fashion in which he successfully sold all his catch. The business man decided to address such talent with an offer of advice. Graciously the fisherman listened as the business man began complimenting and advising him.

"You should start by getting a bigger boat which can hold more fish, then you can work six days a week or so and double if not triple your income." The amused fisherman asked "Then what?"

"Then you could buy another boat, and another, and another until you had a fleet of boats and you could work around the clock." The fisherman said "Then what?"

"Then you could buy a great building in the city, move your family there and continue to grow and expand so you never

have to fish yourself, but rather work all day in your office and over see your massive corporation." "Then what?"

"Then you can retire and move to a quite peaceful little village somewhere and do a little fishing, enjoy fine meals, laugh and sing and spend quality time with your family." Then the business man recognized where the man was, smiled and went away. Source: Unknown Author, cited on several websites.

For me, the first 6 or so months of launching a new business venture have always been incredibly challenging yet very exciting. It is in those first few months that:

- Costly mistakes are easily made as you get to understand your business.
- Customer feedback starts coming back to you, giving you an indication of how your business is perceived by the market place.
- The results of your first marketing campaign are seen.
- All the months you spent planning and researching the business should now bear fruit, either starting to result in the outcomes you were after or giving you a hell of a headache!

For some business owners (luckily this didn't occur to me, but I certainly know of people who went through this), harsh reality sets in as they realize that they were not going to generate revenue as quick as they had planned. As a result, they ran out of money in only a few short months and had to walk away from the business disgruntled and penniless.

Adequate and strategic planning, as well as tight control over your finances, should steer you clear of such oversight and put you onto the growth phase.

As the months pass by you will start falling into routines with your business. You will keep evolving your methods, honing in on ways to create efficiencies and differentiating yourself within the marketplace. With a bit of time word will start spreading about your business and as you improve your marketing and sales techniques chances are you will experience growing demand for your products/services.

As this growth occurs you will experience a new set of challenges and problems that the early months didn't bring. Some of these may include, but are not limited to:

- Too much work, not enough time or resources available.

- Taking action to mediate the above problem could lead to further challenges – e.g. staffing, financial hit.

- Running out of stock or unable to keep up with demand.

- Too much demand for one service or product, not enough for the rest.

- Customer complaints.

- Product faults, service delivery issues.

One of the reasons I love business is the variety of experiences and challenges that come on a daily basis when you run your own show. This can however lead to tricky situations, so always be prepared to think quickly and act fast. The speed of your growth will have a big effect on the challenges you face. This speed is usually determined by your business and life goals, with market forces often influencing in either a positive or negative way.

I wanted Goby to become the largest online business in Australia, selling everything from textbooks to holidays and everything in between to university students across Australia.

I wanted SpindaCorp to become the largest and most exclusive medical recruitment agency in the country.

With both businesses, I wanted to make lots of money with the ultimate aim of building, growing and selling the business. I also wanted to work on the businesses and not in them (this difference will be explained in the time management chapter).

While there is nothing wrong with having such goals (after all dreaming big is conducive to positive energy flowing into your business), the approach taken to achieve such goals can make or break a business. This statement is in fact true no matter what your business goals are, whether you want to become a multinational multimillion dollar venture or stay smaller with the goal of working a few days a week and playing golf the rest of the time.

In my case, Goby was simply not prepared well enough to handle the growth that I pushed to achieve. Everything was done too fast on too big a scale. SpindaCorp was better setup and prepared for the growth, but still the business was not hedged well enough to ride through the issues that came at it. My goals were achievable, evidenced by the strong growth in both businesses. What let me down was the approach I took to make this growth happen. Through these mistakes however I have learnt that in order to achieve sustainable growth in business one must be strategic and focused in the approach taken to grow the business.

So what does this actually mean? Let's take a look at the two businesses this book has focused on, Goby and SpindaCorp, and how a different approach could have possibly prevented the sudden rise and fall they both went through, leading instead to a slower, but more sustainable and stable growth path.

Goby

Actual Approach

The original idea was to sell chiropractic textbooks online to students in Australia. Before we solidified our presence in this market however, we expanded into the medical sector as well. As another opportunity presented itself soon after entering the medical sector we pounced onto this new idea, expanding the product lines and increasing our target market from the relatively niche healthcare sector to a non-niche diverse landscape. We bypassed solidifying our market presence, and we were also rather ignorant to the back end resourcing required to pull off going into the new direction. The outcome of all this: chaotic mess that left

John and I running around in all directions trying to solve problem after problem, eventually culminating in the demise of the whole business.

Alternative Approach

We should have instead held off entering the medical market until we had really secured the chiropractic market and bedded down our processes and procedures. The customer experience should have been continuously enhanced, and the backend operations should have then flowed like clockwork. We would only have entered the medical market once the above was achieved (probably 12 – 18 months later than we actually did), replicating the existing processes to allow for a smooth expansion into this sector. At the same time we should have kept working on creating workflow efficiencies and improving back and front end operations.

As the new expansion settles down, we should have then undertaken the necessary research and business planning to determine what is required of an expansion into the whole student market. New workflows and procedures for the proposed expansion would have to be established, testing them along the way. We would have also been wise to consider a serious capital injection at such a stage. As the procedures and planning is finalized, create a mirror website on which real time, real world testing could be undertaken. This phase would also encompass testing how our systems and the outsourced logistics provider systems marry up and function together. Doing this would pinpoint the issues that we experienced in the actual business, but within the safe walls of the testing phase rather than with real clients!

Initially we would forget about all non educational products (like the CD's, DVD's and telecommunications packages), and focus purely on textbooks and the medical equipment. Whilst we are building Get Healthy and developing and testing the plans for Goby, we would spend a lot more time on building relationships with all of our suppliers – keeping them in the loop with our plans for large scale expansion so that when the idea for Goby is implemented the sudden orders don't hit them out of the blue. A greater emphasis would be placed on understanding the financial aspect of the business and spending would be thought out strategically, as opposed to just spending our profits with no real thought given to it all. Once all planning, research, testing etc is completed, we would launch into Goby. In real terms, this would occur up to 24 months later than our actual launch.

The overall goal of this strategy would be to ensure that the growth of the business is in line with our available funds, our capabilities, our capacity, the back end business processes and market presence. It is vital that the growth does not overpower the actual capabilities of not just our business, but that of our suppliers and outsourced service providers (e.g. logistics).

SpindaCorp

Actual Approach

The idea was to recruit doctors into the Australian medical system. After what was a busy initial 10 months of building the business we decided to put on two staff at the same time, and a few months later expanded our staff numbers with another 3 team members. Throughout this time we kept solidifying our presence in the permanent medical recruitment sector. The procedures were ever changing, but we just kept pushing on, changing our processes to keep in line with the landscape.

Putting on so many staff was a strategy that was completely reliant on all of our contracts coming to fruition, thereby enabling us to realize our full fees from them. To our huge mistake, we were relying on future potential revenue, rather than building the business on the actual available cash in our bank. Thus we ate up our money quickly and turned to an overdraft facility to finance operations. A lot of contracts were being signed at this point in time, giving us a false sense of security. Fast forward a number of months and trouble hits us as a result of the global financial crisis and the heavily changing regulatory requirements. Contracts fell over one after the other, taking the business from hitting over $1 million in revenue in year 2 and making serious profits to a question mark over the viability of the business. We tried to turn the business around by looking at new territories and either selling to or partnering with a bigger firm, but the business runs out of steam and we could no longer operate.

Alternative Approach

Rather than putting on staff in response to an increased workload, a more cost effective short term solution would have been to analyze our workflows and split up the tasks evenly between Stuart and myself. Once we are both at absolute capacity then at this stage outsource parts of the process (predominantly all of the tedious paperwork components) on an as needed basis to someone like a stay at home mum. This would have allowed us to keep focusing on recruitment, business development and general revenue generating activities, rather than wasting around 65% of our time on paperwork. This would have bypassed our need to put on extra recruitment staff, who were much more costly to maintain than a casual worker. Our overheads would have stayed lower for longer and our cash in the bank would have just kept building up.

Putting on extra staff should have not occurred until Stuart and I were completely full with recruitment activities; ideally not in the first 18 months of operation to allow the business to stabilize and cash up. Only one extra person should have been put on at any one time, with additional staff only recruited when existing staff were at 100% capacity and regularly billing. By doing so, when the problems occurred with the global financial crisis and procedures tightened we would have had ample cash and relatively low overheads to change focus and turn to the locum sector. It would have also made us a more appealing buyout or partnership target if that was something we wanted to consider. We would have avoided using an overdraft facility and the worst case could have seen us walk away from the business with money in our pockets, rather than no money and a lot of debt.

Being Strategic

As you can see from my experience, it is essential you remain strategic with your approach to growing your business and constantly remain acutely aware of the actual direction your business is heading in. I've also learnt that whilst it is important to keep positive, one must also regularly don the 'devil's advocate' hat and look at the effects various changes could have on your business. You don't need to over do this, and you don't need to get too paranoid and fixated on what if scenarios, just be aware of these and maneuver your business so as to avoid falling down unexpectedly – doing this could mean the difference between success and failure.

Take the decision in SpindaCorp to put on staff using money that hadn't actually been paid to the business yet, but was in the form of future potential income reliant on certain processes and steps being completed. Had I been less dreamy and more realistic I would have questioned the contracts coming in and would have in advance considered a scenario that assumed not all contracts coming to fruition, based on the trend for the registration environment to change. While only a hypothetical, it would certainly have made me think more logically about how I would cover costs without this income and possibly would have prevented so many staff being put on in any given period.

The message here is simple: **Where possible, avoid spending money you don't have.**

This is where regularly assessing your business and using an ever evolving business plan comes into play. Having an intimate understanding of your industry, factors that influence your market sector and the global world of business will also help you stay on top of trends, potentially enabling you to 'predict' the future and act in advance of potentially business crippling changes.

My top 10 tips for growing businesses:

1. Don't count your chickens before the eggs have hatched! In other words, resist the urge to build your business on potential sales or contracts where payment is subject to work being completed or other requirements being met.

2. Under or over estimate your stock requirements and you will certainly set yourself up for a lot of headaches!

3. Think very carefully about putting on staff; make sure you are financially capable of carrying the extra associated costs and make sure you have the workload to keep them busy.

4. Whatever service or product you have sold your customers on make sure you can deliver on your promises.

5. Always keep a financial buffer in your bank account to help you ride through slower times.

6. Build strong relationships with your suppliers.

7. Refer to your business plan regularly and use it to steer the direction of your business.

8. Understand your finances and regularly monitor the financial health of your venture.

9. Don't spend unnecessarily.

10. Keep re-investing in all aspects of the business, from bettering the skills of your staff to the utilization of technology to drive efficiency.

Lessons on Time Management

Mr. T (no, not that one, this is an imaginary office worker) and Mr. H are rivals in the same office, vying for a promotion that is coming up. One of the main factors that will decide which of the two will get the promotion plus the hefty salary rise is productivity.

"It's in the bag," says Mr. H, "I can type like the wind while old Mr. T plods on with his tongue out." And with this, Mr. H started typing away very quickly.

But while Mr. H sped away, Mr. T brought into play all of his time management skills and his progress was steady, if slower than that of Mr. H. He studied his to do list and prioritized his workload. In doing this he took into consideration the fact that workers are generally more productive in the morning when they are fresher, so he put the more strenuous jobs at the top of the list so that he would have the energy to tackle them.

Mr. H, on the other hand, just sped through one job after another, sometimes showing off his multitasking skills by doing two at once and not bothering to prioritize his workload. He believed himself to be so far ahead of Mr. T that when he answered his phone to Jenny from admin, he spent time chatting her up. His rival, however, had set up an automated email reply and answer phone message to tell callers that he would be unavailable for the whole of that day.

Mr. T continued to plod on methodically and carefully, sticking to each task until it was completed before moving on to the next one, well aware that switching between jobs is counter-productive in the long run.

Finally Mr. H hung up the phone and he was startled to see that he was now actually behind Mr. T. Not only that, he also had several unfinished tasks because he didn't stick to doing one at a time. Just as Mr. T finished the last of his tasks the boss entered and Mr. H was still frantically typing away. After checking their respective efforts, the boss awarded Mr. T the promotion, while Mr. H took a few weeks' sick leave, suffering from burnout. "I didn't want the job anyway, there's a much nicer view from this window," he said as he left the office, demonstrating that sour grapes still have a place in the modern world. Source: www.micrsofttraining.net

In the business or on the business?

I want to discuss something very important with you: The difference between working in the business and working on the business.

Do you fully understand the difference between the two and the importance this has on the potential success of you and your business? In really simple terms, when you are working *in* the business you are packaging the goods to your customers, with not having much time for business building activities. When you are working *on* the business, your team does the packaging, while you are out with clients negotiating new deals, actively working towards further growth, innovating and shaping the course of your business.

Ultimately as the head of the business you want to get to a stage where you can step out of the daily inner workings, handing that to your managers and team so that you can focus on the bigger picture.

While it's enjoyable working in your own business, as things get busy and your growth takes off, being pulled away from working on the business can stunt your growth. Getting to the point however when you can truly step into the 'on' role from the 'in' role will take time and perseverance.

So why am I telling you about this under the time management section?

I've been watching a friend build and grow his business for many years now. Through a huge amount of hard work and dedication he has built the business to become a profitable venture that generates him a very nice income. His goal however has always been to grow the business huge, to become a large national company that is the leader in his industry and of course to make him very wealthy along the way. There is however one obstacle preventing him from achieving this: he is constantly being drawn back into the inner workings of the business, to work on his factory floor, making him too time poor to dedicate the energy and focus required to take the company to the next level. As a result, the business is stagnating and his frustration and impatience is growing. Time and time again I tell him to change his ways, to be smarter with the way he spends his time and energy within his business. He won't listen though, and instead his business is plateauing with no real growth forecast for the future.

The lesson in this is simple: **mismanage your time and resources, and your business will suffer.**

Time Factor – When 24 hours in a day is not enough

As your business takes off and demand for your services/products picks up you will face a tough truth: success in business comes at a price – namely in the form of time and energy. It is not uncommon for business owners to be working 7 day weeks and very long hours where the days seem to blend together and caffeine becomes a best friend.

While it can be quite exhilarating being so busy in your own business, the problems that come with too much work and not enough time for anything else can have a significant negative impact on your personal health and life. Stress from too much work put me in hospital in my early 20's with severe stomach problems, and at the age of 30 I had a heart attack scare that really made me realize I need to slow down. Being successful in business is great, but I ask you this: what's the point if you can't enjoy the success in good health with your family and friends?

Nowadays I make it my priority to not allow business and work interfere with my private life. I ensure that even during busy periods I set aside time for myself, my family and friends, and I make sure that this time is quality – that is, I am there 100% and not taking business call after business call or checking my emails every 5 minutes. You may be surprised just how much business can take over one's life – I even worked on my wedding day and almost every day on our honeymoon (luckily for me my wife is understanding, but it doesn't mean she was happy with this!).

Looking back at your time problem, take a moment out, grab a pen and large paper and do the following:

1. Take apart your work days, and examine exactly how you spend your time. List the activities and approximate time you spend on these. Do you see any wasted time or ways you could reschedule your tasks to be more efficient?

2. Order the above in a list, starting with activities that take up most of your time. Break down each task into all of its components. Make sure to capture all of the pieces of the puzzle.

3. Put on your strategy hat and look at what you have written down. Do you see unnecessary steps? Do you see how you could perform tasks differently to get the required result in a more efficient manner? If nothing can be changed, are there tasks that you could outsource?

Having completed similar tasks both within my companies and whilst working for someone else, I would be surprised if you found nothing helpful that could immediately benefit your business.

Now, I want you to go back to the beginning of this chapter and re-read the story of Mr. T and Mr. H. There is an important lesson in this, and it is one that I personally live by every day. If you have a whole heap of things to do at any one time, then before you start working on any of the activities spend a few minutes planning out a to do list. Write down the activities, rank them in order of importance, then either allocate time to each activity (usually when an activity is so large that it will take days/weeks/months to complete) or just start working through the list in order of importance, crossing off each completed item as you go along. I know this sounds simplistic, but this simple activity will save you time, money and energy in the long run! I do this every day and helps me keep on top of a very hectic workload, so I am proof that it works.

There will however come a point when you are putting in as much time as you can, you have completed the above exercise a couple times and yet your workload demands still exceed your capacity.

To continue growing and meeting client expectations you will now need to look at building on your available resources and making strategic growth-focused decisions.

Ways to free up your 'on the business' time at this stage could include:

- Investing in staff.

- Outsource parts of your work.

- Upgrade your machinery.

- Invest in new technologies that can cut down on procedures, creating efficiencies.

- Review your processes and ensure they are running as efficiently as possible.

Of all of the above, making the decision to invest in staff is one of the biggest decisions you can make in your business. It is a decision that can make or break a business and one that will bring you plenty of new challenges......

Lessons on Staffing

Reaching the end of a job interview, the human resources representative asked a young engineer fresh out of MIT, "And what starting salary were you looking for?"

The engineer said, "In the neighbourhood of $150,000 a year, depending on the benefits package."

The interviewer said, "Well, what would you say to a package of five-weeks vacation, full medical and dental, company matching retirement fund to 50 percent of salary, and a company car leased every two years, say, a red Corvette?"

The engineer sat up straight and said, "Wow! Are you kidding?"

And the interviewer replied, "Yeah, but you started it." Source: www.commoninterview.com

A big moment in the life of any business is when the first employee is hired. Before you tell the world however of your vacancy, there are a number of things to consider and do:

1. Do you know the exact role this person will play within your organization, including all of the tasks they will complete? Make sure to clearly

document this in a position description that your new starter can refer to.

2. Once you are able to answer yes to Q1, looking at your current workload and expected workload in the coming 6 months, how much time do you need this person to spend in your business?

3. Depending on how you bring on staff (e.g. permanent fulltime vs. casual part time vs. contractors etc), different obligations will need to be met by you as the employer. Are you aware of these and how they will affect your business? Visit the Fair Work Australia website for more information (www.fairwork.gov.au).

4. Do you currently have enough funds in the bank to fully cover the running costs of your business (including your staff wages and your wages) for a minimum of 3 months? This is playing devil's advocate but should anything happen and your revenue dips, having this as a backup could save your business. Remember, it is one thing to not pay yourself in lean times (which I have done on many occasions), but it's also another thing to not have funds to pay your staff.

5. Following on from point 4, be mindful that once staff are in the picture you get paid last.

When the first two consultants started with me at SpindaCorp I found myself breathing a big sigh of relief as I could finally offload my massive workload. I had more time to work on the business, spending more time with clients rather than getting bogged down on the paperwork side of things. By luck, there was enough work on the table for the new starters, but had that not been the case I would have quickly found myself carrying the costs for someone to be bored, taking months to build their work up. Later as it got busy again I reacted swiftly with staffing, thinking it was the only solution to my time dilemma, rather than looking at things with a more long term approach and really analyzing who was doing what function in the business. In hindsight things could have been re-jigged or reallocated, avoiding the need to spend more money on staff. I broke my own rule on rushing things several times and bypassed analyzing how my staff spent their time. This of course was to my detriment only months down the track.

Recruitment

Putting aside the financial considerations of bringing staff onboard, rushing the recruitment process is a foolish endeavor. A well thought out and planned recruitment strategy will pay off over and over in the form of well chosen staff who will be a good fit and become an asset to your organization.

I liken the creation and running of a recruitment campaign to that of a marketing campaign. In the case of recruitment your business is the product, your potential employees are the customers. The goal is to make your company as attractive as possible to the candidate pool so as to give you the best chance to attract the best pool of candidates to select from.

Before you start actively recruiting, several things need to be done:

1. Know the exact role of the new employee within your organization and draw up a detailed position description.

2. Similar to marketing, it is important to understand your target market.

    o Who do you want to attract to your business?

    o What drives and motivates them?

    o What are their skills?

A mind map can be useful for this.

3. What tools are available to market your vacancy? Again, I recommend the creation of a mind map for this.

4. Table the above (similar to your marketing medium table), listing media type and cost.

5. Decide on your campaign.

The Campaign and Selection Process

Whether you are planning a campaign to recruit professionals to your team or a 16 year old to man the cash register and pack your shelves, your campaign strategy should follow a similar path:

1. Writing ads
2. Sorting CVs
3. Interviews
4. Contracts

Of course these will vary greatly with your hiring needs.

Let's compare your campaign to recruit a 16 year old to pack shelves and clean floors in your store, versus your campaign to recruit a 43 year old medical doctor to work in your clinic:

Realities of Business: Misadventures and Lessons Learnt

Campaign Step	Store Hand	Medical Doctor
Writing Your Advert	Short, to the point, often just a few lines long. Advert might even be as simple as a 'Staff Wanted' sign in your shop window.	In depth, well written advert detailing information such as your clinic, scope of work, opportunity on offer etc. Ad needs to read well, be grammatically correct and sound professional.
Sorting CVs	In general the less professional the role, the shorter the CV will be and the easier for you to read through and understand. Refer to your position description and sort your CVs in order from best matching to least matching your selection criteria and requirements.	The more professional the role, the longer and more complex a CV can become. Knowing how to sift through pages of information and understanding this information is important in order for you to be able to make accurate decisions at this stage. Use your position description to help sort through the CVs and putting them in order from best matching to least.
Interviews	Irrespective of how simple the role may be, always interview candidates before making the decision to offer	Interviewing for more complex professional roles will require you to prepare a well thought out line of

		them a job. Use your position description as the guide for your line of questioning and listen carefully to their answers, paying attention to tone, body language and sentence use. Also watch out for their presentation, promptness in attending the interview and their enthusiasm. With a simple role usually one interview will suffice.	questioning well in advance of the interview. As with an interview for any role, watch out for body language, tone, sentence use, enthusiasm and presentation and listen carefully to the candidate's response to your questions. In most cases you will need two or three interviews with the one candidate in order to give you the best overview of that candidate. You may also want to put them through psychometric assessments and even give them a vocational test to complete. Again, all this depends on the requirements of the role.
Contracts		If you are happy with the candidate you may decide to hire them on the spot. Always get them to sign an employment contract, even if it's for a part time shelf packing role. The contract for simple roles need not be long or complicated, just make sure it outlines the important expectations you	The process of negotiating and agreeing on the terms of contract for a professional role can take a bit of going back and forth. In most cases you will be able to reach an agreement easily, provided you are being fair with what you are offering and the candidate is being realistic. Watch out for

	have and also includes the benefits provided to your new employee.	unrealistic candidates and over the top requests! For professional roles have employment contracts drawn up by your solicitor – better to be well prepared than to be stung down the track by unscrupulous employees.

My tips for the campaign and selection process:

- Create your ads with your target market in mind. Don't overcomplicate things, keep them simple where possible.

- Your ads represent your company. This is particularly important for senior/professional roles; so remember to use ads to make your company look attractive to prospective candidates.

- When sorting through CVs, rank candidates based on the number of position description requirements you can tick off on their CV.

- Prepare your interview questions based on your position description and your expectations of the role.

- During the interview take note of the candidates:

  - Timeliness

  - Presentation

  - Body language

  - Tone

  - Language used

  - Responses to your questions

  - Confidence and enthusiasm

- For more professional roles you may wish to conduct multiple interviews, maybe even put candidates through assessments. Use this time with the candidate to get to know the real person. Look out for clues that may indicate that the candidate is lying or covering something up. Multiple interviews are great for catching out candidates or for breaking down barriers.

- Listen to your instincts. I know this sounds corny, but your gut instincts are usually correct. I made the mistake of ignoring my instincts on a couple of occasions in my business career, especially during the recruitment stage, and have regretted it down the track. If something doesn't add up with a candidate, don't dismiss it – ask more questions and if you still feel hesitant then put them aside and look at others.

- I have had candidates come through with flying colors in the interviews, only to have the whole thing unravel when it came time to negotiate their contract. Be very cautious of candidates who are inflexible and overly demanding at this stage. Again, I have made the mistake of bending over backwards for demanding candidates, only to find them an absolute nightmare to manage once employed. Having said this, there is nothing wrong with a bit of to and fro when negotiating contracts. In fact, I appreciate it when candidates are willing to push me for more, as long as they are realistic with their expectations and not overly cocky or arrogant. Remember, if they are hard work before you have even employed them, what they will be like once they have the job?!

- Make sure that whatever you discuss and agree to with your candidate goes into the employment contract and is signed by the candidate.

- Don't rush the recruitment process. Having employed dozens of staff over the years I have learned it's best to wait an extra month or two for the right person rather than accept someone out of desperation. Know what you are after in a person and be clear with the role and its expectations from the beginning to avoid any misunderstandings.

As you can see, I am now very process oriented with staffing, and for me all the right boxes need to be ticked before I am willing to take someone on. I only want the right person working on my teams, and so should you.

Induction

The last step remaining in the recruitment of staff is inducting your new person into your company. You have gone through the recruitment process, have agreed on the terms of employment and they are ready to join your business. Even if the person is experienced and has been in a similar role previously, don't assume that from day one they will step into the role and know everything. In fact, I have found induction especially important with experienced people so that I can see just how they work and how they carry out tasks. You may find them completing work totally differently to how you want it done, or even better yet, they may show you a technique that could improve your efficiency.

The induction process for someone stepping into a new role to which they have had limited exposure to before (e.g. a school leaver starting their first job or an experienced recruiter who has been working in blue collar, now moving into white collar sectors) should result in the employee understanding their role, responsibilities and demonstrating competence at completing the required tasks without you needing to constantly hold their hands. In some cases this may take a few days; in others it may be a gradual 3 month process. Induction for an experienced person is much simpler, and may be as easy as you watching them work for a day, or you reviewing their work for the first week or two to ensure consistency, accuracy and the way you want things done is understood by your employee.

I remember stepping into my first medical sales job and feeling quite overwhelmed by the complexity of the role. I was hoping to be trained up before being sent out into the field, but to my disappointment induction only consisted of a 5 minute tour of the office. I was shown the product catalogue library and told to 'get on with it'. It's a good thing that I work well under pressure, as the sink or swim approach does not fare well with everyone! Looking back now with the experience I have had developing teams, I can say with 100% certainty that I would have become a fully productive member of the team and making less mistakes much sooner had there been a solid induction process in place to train me up on the products and their use. My second role in the same industry saw me face a very structured induction process that lasted around 8 weeks. There was heavy emphasis placed on product training, so much so that I even spent 2 weeks in the US at the company's headquarters undertaking an intensive training course. I stepped into this role with a lot more confidence, and had as strong an understanding of my new range of products after 8 weeks as I had gained after about 6 months with the previous employer.

Your Role

With your business consisting of more than just you (and your business partner if you have one), the role you play will transform from that of pure business owner to that of business owner, manager, leader and mentor. Your team will rely on you for guidance and support, for motivation and strength during tough times. Managing individuals is a highly debated topic, with many thoughts and theorems existing on the matter.

In reality, management is a complex interplay of psychology, authority, personalities and circumstances. True leaders deploy management styles based on the current situation and prevailing needs. A number of management styles exist in every workplace; just think of your previous employers. Can you identify a person in charge who has fallen into one or more of these common styles:

- **Democratic:** Employees are allowed and encouraged to take part in decision making, with a majority votes approach to issues. Communication is open and flowing in two directions: top down and bottom up. This is a good style to turn to when making complex decisions as it opens up the floor to a greater mix of skills and experience. Negatives with this style is the potential to slow down decision making processes and the fact that what is best for everyone is not always the right decision for the business.

- **Autocratic:** In this style the manager makes all decisions unilaterally and without regard for their team. Orders are dictated to staff, and the manager is the one in control of the situation. Unlike democratic styles, decisions are made quickly, projecting a confident image of the business and often enabling a quicker turnaround time for projects. Some of the negatives include potentially decreased team motivation and increased staff turnover due to people feeling undervalued and disregarded, or overdependence by staff on their manager, requiring greater supervision and hand holding.

- **Paternalistic:** Similar to Autocratic in that it is a very dictatorial style as this type of manager still makes decisions predominantly on their own. The main difference however lies in the decision making process, as it now takes into account not just the needs of the business, but that of their employees' well being and personal needs.

- **Laissez Faire:** This is a very hands off style which sees managers give staff complete freedom to complete tasks as they see fit, often with little managerial direction. Delegation is at the heart of this style. Having said this, without direct leadership staff can feel lost and teams veering away from the original goals. Interestingly this approach can on the other hand increase staff motivation as people feel a greater sense of responsibility. This is a particularly good style to be used with highly experienced, motivated individuals.

Some of the above styles even have sub styles within the main style, e.g. democratic can be permissive or directive. Of course, the above styles are not all encompassing – they are just the main styles usually discussed.

Putting all categories aside, my take on the role of a business owner/manager from a staffing point of view is to:

- Positively motivate their team.
- Instill a sense of ownership with individual team members, by promoting entrepreneurship, creativity and ingenuity.
- Guide and direct the team towards the required goals whilst enabling individual autonomy.
- Promote healthy group discussions on the direction the business is heading in, creating further team buy in.
- Make strategic, well thought out decisions succinctly, then to take responsibility for those decisions.
- Promote all wins.

- Performance manage poor performers in an appropriate manner.
- Reward and acknowledge good performers.

As a business owner and manager my personal style has always been to lead by example, to treat all of my staff as equals and as adults, always expecting 110% from everyone including myself, and promoting a round table environment where my staff are involved with certain business decisions. It's fair to say that I tend to gravitate towards democracy in my businesses. Having said this, I am also Autocratic when necessary and will come down hard on staff and performance manage them – either getting them back in line with my expectations or firing them after a period of close performance management.

Managing and leading staff is a challenging but very satisfying and rewarding task. As your team grows during the life of your business you will face situations with staff that will test your strength and you may even face situations you never even thought of. No doubt at times you will want to tear your hair out in frustration with your team. Other times you will have to be strong as you act on the decision to fire a staff member. Whatever the situation, you must learn to be flexible, understanding, patient and directive if you want to build successful relationships with your staff.

At the end of the day though, my message to you on leadership and management is simple: **Treat your staff how you would want to be treated by your manager.**

Lessons on Financial Management

In a field one summer's day a Grasshopper was hopping about, chirping and singing to its heart's content. An Ant passed by, bearing along with great toil an ear of corn he was taking to the nest.

"Why not come and chat with me," said the Grasshopper, "instead of toiling and moiling in that way?"

"I am helping to lay up food for the winter," said the Ant, "and recommend you to do the same."

"Why bother about winter?" said the Grasshopper; "we have got plenty of food at present." But the Ant went on its way and continued its toil. When the winter came the Grasshopper had no food and found itself dying of hunger, while every day it saw the ants distributing corn and grain from the stores they had collected in the summer. Then the Grasshopper knew: it is best to prepare for the days of necessity. – Aesop

Money Matters – Understanding Finance

I used to be a big picture person and struggled with the finer detail in things. As a result I have made some costly mistakes and have since learnt to be pedantic and detail oriented with my business dealings, especially when it comes to financial matters.

Cash is at the heart of your business: without cash your business won't be in existence. It is thus vital that you make it your daily goal to know exactly how your business is tracking financially at any point in time.

I've been lucky enough to have always enjoyed math's, so working with numbers in my businesses has never been an issue. I do however know that I am an oddity, so chances are that at first you may feel a little daunted by the financial side of your venture. Once you get your head around the basics though you will find it can become quite a breeze.

Before heading into the details I would like to make three suggestions that will make your life much easier:

1. **Invest the time to learn how to use spread sheets.** Spend a few hours playing with spread sheeting software and you will see just what powerful tools these are for business. In particular, look at how to create and use formulas for simple and multi number calculations.

2. **Utilize the services of a book keeper.** A small fee each month will ensure all of your business financial documents are up to date and in order. This is especially useful if you are like me and hate the paperwork related to taxation, expenses, receipt collection, etc. They can also handle all your staff related wage payments and superannuation.

3. **If you haven't already done so, source yourself a good accountant.** Apart from helping you come tax time, they can give you valuable advice on how to best utilize legal taxation rules to your advantage and how to work your cash to your advantage.

Terminologies

For the real world small business there is no need to overcomplicate business financials. The main terminologies you need to understand and use are:

- **Revenue:** The actual dollars received for your goods and/or services over a period of time.
- **Expenses:** Costs associated with the operation of your business but not including company tax.
- **EBIT (Earnings Before Interest and Tax):** The profit remaining once you take the expenses out

of your revenue, but have not taken company taxes or bank interest amounts into consideration.

- **NET Profit:** The amount of money left over after all expenses (including taxes and interest charges) have been taken out of your revenue. *This is what you are chasing* and it is this figure that you want in constant strong positive.

Pricing Models

As with many things, it took a few mistakes before I realized just how important it is to get pricing right for the overall success of a business.

Come in too low with your prices and you may find yourself making little or no money. Come in too high, and although your profit margins will have improved, you may find yourself sitting around, twiddling your thumb as your customers go somewhere cheaper.

So what are the factors you need to bear in mind when setting prices, and how do you determine the price for a product or service?

Price Positioning

If you set a **low** price:

- You may impact on the customers' perception of quality, irrespective of true quality.
- A greater volume of sales is needed to generate profit and to cover your whole of business running costs.
- Can your business sustain a low price, high volume model?
- Can you ensure a consistently high volume of sales?

If you set a **high** price:

- You may potentially lose customers to other businesses, often irrespective of quality.
- A lower volume of sales is needed to turn a profit and cover your whole of business expenses, but it may also mean it will be harder to convince customers to buy from you.
- Can you sustain your business if you have priced at the high end of the market?
- Will there be enough demand for the high cost products/services?

Pricing needs to be flexible enough to allow you to change according to market conditions, without impacting too much on your ability to cover your business expenses and generate decent profits. How you price your products/services will affect not only your profit margins and sales volumes, but also your branding and customer perception of the inherent value of your offerings. Let's take a look at an example of where I played with different pricing levels in SpindaCorp, only to have clients then question the service the business was offering.

Setting the price levels for SpindaCorp services was not difficult as I knew the industry well enough and had researched my competition to know who was charging what. To start with, I wanted to position SpindaCorp as an agency that provided high quality service offerings on a mid-tier pricing structure – I didn't want to enter too high, because I wanted to gain quick momentum in making placements and thus generating revenue. Initially all was well and clients rarely questioned the pricing. Then, just to try something different, Stuart and I decided to trial run a 'sale event' – and for one month we offered candidates at heavily discounted rates. A $9,000 fee was reduced to $2,000. A $15,000 fee was reduced to $5,000 and so on. Interestingly, that month we made absolutely no placements, and in fact we had a number of clients raise questions and show concern as to why we would discount such services. So the lesson was learnt, and that was the last and only time in SpindaCorp that we ran any form of discounting or special sales campaigns. Shortly after this I raised the prices across the board, taking for example a $30,000 fee to $36,000. And you know what? Not one client complained, and the business was not impacted negatively in any way at all. Of course, if I had kept putting up prices eventually a ceiling would have been hit, after which point clients would have pushed back and raised concerns over the value they were getting.

Calculating Pricing

The goal of any business is to return a profit for its owners and shareholders. With this in mind, your pricing needs to contain sufficient margins to:

1. Cover your costs associated with the product/service.

2. Pay for the cost of running your business.

3. Generate profits.

So, in order to be able to work out your pricing you need to know roughly what your expenses will be for the year ahead, and you also need to know how much the product or service will cost you per unit (and not just a wholesale price but all associated costs such as shipping, packaging etc). From here, it will be a bit of experimentation on your part in order to find that 'optimum pricing' level – the price that will return you the maximum profit generating potential which the customers are still willing to pay.

You can use a number of methods to calculate your pricing, including:

- **Cost Plus** – This is the standard method of marking up pricing using a percentage level, e.g. 10% markup on cost.

- **Market Rate** – Price in line with your competitors.

- **Sliding Scale** – Different price depending on volumes/timeframes/commitments.

- **Value Based** – Perceived value by the customer.

In reality you will probably find yourself using a combination of the above. For Goby, I used the Cost Plus and Sliding Scale methods. For SpindaCorp, I used Market Rate combined with a Value Based approach.

Following on from this, look at the diagram below:

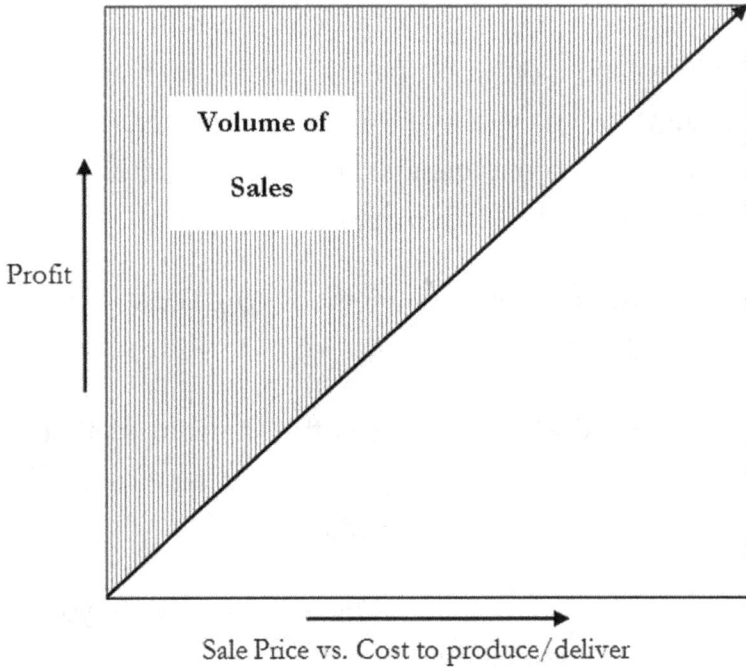

Sale Price vs. Cost to produce/deliver

As you can see, increasing your Sale Price vs. Cost to produce/deliver ratio will increase your profit margins. At the same time, you can see that the lower the Sale Price vs. Cost to produce/deliver ratio, the greater volume of sales are required to generate the same profits.

Here are some of my tips for pricing:

- Start off by knowing your true business costs and the true costs to produce your product or service offerings. Forecast out and make sure you can generate enough sales to cover these costs and return a decent profit.

- Research pricing by finding out what your competitors are doing. Visit their stores. Ring around and ask for quotes. Check out their website. Armed with this information you can truly work on being competitive yet sustainable and profitable with your pricing.

- In addition, when marketing/promoting/selling your products, you can create a diversion away from a price focus towards a value based focus. This technique enables customers to see the value and benefits of your products/service to them, and puts pricing second to the importance of this value to the customer. I have used this technique numerous times in many sales calls, and have found that once a value is identified for a customer, it is relatively easy to convince them on your pricing (except of course where your price is totally unrealistic, in which case no amount of value marketing or selling will get you sales).

- Resist the urge to discount. If your business generated $200,000 revenue selling 5,000 items at $40 each, discount by 10% and you will need an additional 11% in sales to reach the same profit as before. Discount by 20% on the same amounts, and you will need to generate an additional 25% in sales to be at the original profit margins. The greater your discounting, the greater your sales volume needs to increase by in order to generate the same profit as a no discount scenario.

- As outlined above, sell the benefits of your offerings, and don't focus on pricing.

Tracking your Financials

As I mentioned at the beginning of this chapter, it is vital that you make it your daily business to know exactly how your business is tracking financially. Staying on top of the figures regularly will enable you to pick up trends and spot areas of bleed before things get out of control.

How you track your financials is totally your decision. My personal preference is to have my book keeper regularly update all financial records into a financial product such as Xero ™, MYOB™ or QUICKEN™, while at the same time I use a spreadsheet containing my forecasted, budgeted and actual expenses, revenue and

EBIT for tracking purposes. Turning to a financial program for record keeping enables my business taxation to be handled quickly and efficiently, and allows me (or my bookkeeper) to easily generate accurate Profit and Loss (P&L) reports.

In the Goby days my financial management was ad hoc at best; SpindaCorp was run a lot tighter as I used spreadsheets on a daily basis. You need to assess your own situation and come up with an easy system that you stick to religiously. For me in my current ventures pedantic is the word as I update my spreadsheet every day, documenting revenue and expenses for the day which automatically (using formulas) give me an update of my revenue, expenses and EBIT for the week, month and Year To Date (YTD).

As indicated above, I use financial spreadsheets religiously in my businesses, with the main ones being:

1. **Budgets (Revenue and Expense):** This is the financial plan of how much money you want to make and spend. If you have a team, their budget is a plan of targets they have to achieve in order to qualify for bonuses (where relevant) and of course it's your tool to measure performance against.

2. **Cashflow Forecast:** This is the financial result you think you will achieve. The difference between budget and cashflow forecast is in the way they are utilized. Your budget should be set at the beginning of the financial year (FY), preferably left untouched for the year, and should be a challenging goal for you and your team to reach towards. Your cashflow forecast on the other hand is fluid and should change with the needs of the business and market environment. While you aim to hit your budget, use your forecast to improve on business costs and maximize the revenue generating potential of you and your team.

3. **P&L:** These are the real figures – put simply this is how much money actually came in and how much money went out.

Just creating these spreadsheets in the first place is a good start, but it's a futile exercise unless you actually use them regularly. And by regularly, I mean every week (of course this is in the ideal world, but you should at least run through your financial analysis every month).

Here is how I use these tools:

End of each month

- Compare my forecasted revenue, expenses and EBIT for the past month with the actuals in the P&L.

- Compare my budget for revenue, expenses and EBIT with the actuals in the P&L.

- Create my forecast for the coming month, taking into account my budget goals and the P&L figures from prior months.

As I undertake the above activities I take note of any discrepancies between the forecast, budget and P&L figures. I hone in on major discrepancies and find a reason for these. During these monthly reviews I also look back historically at YTD for the prior financial year and at the figures for the current FY. This allows me to notice any trends as they begin to form and allows me to take corrective actions in time.

Beginning of each week

- I complete a similar exercise to my monthly analysis, but on a smaller scale.

- I look at prior week figures, update my actuals and compare them to my forecast and budget.

- From a forecasting point of view I look at the week ahead, and make changes to my revenue and expense lines if I feel that the coming week will bring changes that will affect my initial forecast figures.

- As I make the above changes I attach notes to my spreadsheet where the changes are made, which I use at the end of the month to see where changes occurred and the reasons for them.

Running my financials this way may seem over analytical, but it gives me the ability (especially over time as data starts to build up) to:

1. Know accurately what the financial health of the business is at any point in time.

2. Pick up any patterns that may have a direct future impact on my business and spot potential issues before they escalate out of control.

3. Forecast my expenses with greater accuracy, thus giving me greater control of my money and the ability to jump at opportunities when they arise.

After a bit of practice this weekly activity shouldn't take more than a couple of hours to complete.

Having strong knowledge of this information will prevent you from sailing in the dark and hiding away from the real financial health of your business. With this in mind, let's now look at some of these components in more detail.

Budgets

Purpose

To give you revenue targets to work towards and to help keep your expenses in line with available funds, thus helping you sustain the viability of your business. Budgets are also tools used to monitor, motivate and incentivize teams and individuals.

I have personally used two different types of budgets in my businesses: company budgets and team budgets.

Company Budget

This is the rolled up budget for your whole business. In the early stages of business where you don't have staff or in a business where your staff don't require a budget, this is the only one you need to worry about.

Your budget should be as detailed and as accurate as possible and should include your:

- Target Revenue (not including taxes such as the GST)

- Expenses – captured under main headings and subheadings

- EBIT

Have a look at my example below (note this example is for 3 months only, versus the usual 12 months):

	July	August	September	TOTAL
Revenue				
Product Line 1	$72,000.00	$89,000.00	$55,000.00	**$216,000.00**
Product Line 2	210,000.00	2,000.00	36,000.00	**$248,000.00**
Service Line 1	6,000.00	12,000.00	8,000.00	**$26,000.00**
Total Revenue	*288,000.00*	*103,000.00*	*99,000.00*	*490,000.00*

Realities of Business: Misadventures and Lessons Learnt

Expenses				
Salaries and Wages - Full-time	42,000.00	44,000.00	41,500.00	127,500.00
Annual Leave	1,000.00	1,200.00	1,000.00	3,200.00
Long Service Leave	120.00	135.00	123.00	378.00
Sick Leave	165.00	180.00	173.00	518.00
Overtime	0.00	986.00	0.00	986.00
Salaries and Wages	43,285.00	46,501.00	42,796.00	132,582.00
Bonuses	250.00	300.00	250.00	800.00
Payroll Tax	980.00	1,120.00	1,076.00	3,176.00
Superannuation	1,000.00	1,100.00	1,050.00	3,150.00
Worker's Compensation	34.00	46.00	42.00	122.00

On costs	2,014.00	2,266.00	2,168.00	6,448.00
Staff Uniforms	560.00	124.00	0.00	684.00
Staff Amenities	220.00	220.00	220.00	660.00
Other Salary	998.00	842.00	243.00	2,083.00
Redundancy Payments	0.00	0.00	0.00	0.00
Other Termination Costs	0.00	0.00	0.00	0.00
Termination Costs	0.00	0.00	0.00	0.00
Agency Fees	0.00	0.00	0.00	0.00
Staff Advertising – Recruitment	250.00	250.00	0.00	500.00
Recruitment Costs	250.00	250.00	0.00	500.00

Training	500.00	150.00	400.00	1,050.00
Total Staff	47,297.00	50,309.00	45,857.00	143,463.00
Car Parking	25.00	0.00	40.00	65.00
Electricity, Water & Gas	200.00	200.00	200.00	600.00
Repairs & Maintenance	0.00	300.00	0.00	300.00
Rent Premises	1,200.00	1,400.00	1,200.00	3,800.00
Rates & Taxes	200.00	200.00	200.00	600.00
Office Cleaning	150.00	150.00	150.00	450.00
Other Office Expenses	0.00	0.00	0.00	0.00
Total Premises	1,979.00	2,343.00	2,032.00	6,354.00

Internet	200.00	200.00	200.00	**600.00**
Phone – Fixed	100.00	100.00	100.00	**300.00**
Phone – Mobile	400.00	400.00	400.00	**1,200.00**
Postage, Freight & Couriers	20.00	20.00	20.00	**60.00**
Total Communications	**870.00**	**870.00**	**870.00**	**2,610.00**
Accommodation & Meals	0.00	400.00	600.00	**1,000.00**
Airfares	0.00	800.00	800.00	**1,600.00**
Other Travel Expenses	376.00	100.00	209.00	**685.00**
Travel Away Allowance	0.00	300.00	0.00	**300.00**
Travel & Accommodation	**376.00**	**1,600.00**	**1,609.00**	**3,585.00**

Entertainment – Non Staff	400.00	400.00	400.00	**1,200.00**
Entertainment – Staff	600.00	600.00	600.00	**1,800.00**
Entertainment	1,000.00	1,000.00	1,000.00	3,000.00
Total Travel, Accommodation & Entertainment	1,376.00	2,600.00	2,609.00	6,585.00
Motor Vehicle Car Hire	0.00	200.00	0.00	**200.00**
Motor Vehicle Operating Expenses	150.00	150.00	150.00	**450.00**
Motor Vehicle Insurance & Excess	100.00	100.00	100.00	**300.00**
Motor Vehicle Leases	2,000.00	2,000.00	2,000.00	**6,000.00**
Motor Vehicle Costs	2,250.00	2,450.00	2,250.00	6,950.00

Equipment Minor<$1000	3,500.00	0.00	0.00	**3,500.00**
Equipment Costs Leasing	700.00	600.00	700.00	**2,000.00**
Equipment – Repair & Maintenance	50.00	50.00	50.00	**150.00**
Equipment Costs	**4,250.00**	**650.00**	**750.00**	**5,650.00**
Total Motor Vehicle & Equipment	**6,500.00**	**3,100.00**	**3,000.00**	**12,600.00**
Legal / Fees	3,050.00	0.00	0.00	**3,050.00**
Accounting Fees	980.00	0.00	0.00	**980.00**
Bank Charges	10.00	10.00	10.00	**30.00**
Provision for Doubtful Debts	0.00	(1,200.00)	(500.00)	**(1,700.00)**
Finance Application Fees	0.00	25.00	0.00	**25.00**

Realities of Business: Misadventures and Lessons Learnt

Any Other Financials	0.00	0.00	0.00	0.00
Financial Expenses	4,040.00	(1,156.00)	(485.00)	2,398.00
Insurance Professional Indemnity	56.00	60.00	56.00	172.00
Insurance Public Liability	34.00	34.00	34.00	102.00
Insurance – Other	23.00	23.00	23.00	69.00
Insurance	113.00	117.00	113.00	343.00
Total Financial Expenses	4,153.00	(1,039.00)	(372.00)	2,741.00
Donations	150.00	150.00	150.00	450.00
Printing, Stationery & Office Supplies	300.00	200.00	450.00	950.00
Memberships, Subscriptions &	135.00	135.00	135.00	405.00

Realities of Business: Misadventures and Lessons Learnt

Publications				
Waste Destruction	20.00	20.00	20.00	**60.00**
Administration	**605.00**	**561.00**	**755.00**	**1,921.00**
Hardware Consumables	300.00	400.00	300.00	**1,000.00**
Software Costs	150.00	150.00	150.00	**450.00**
Website Development & Maintenance	600.00	600.00	600.00	**1,800.00**
Information Technology	**1,050.00**	**1,450.00**	**1,050.00**	**3,550.00**
Advertising, Design and Brochures	2,500.00	0.00	0.00	**2,500.00**
Conferences & Seminars	0.00	0.00	0.00	**0.00**
Promotional Expenses	1,000.00	1,000.00	1,000.00	**3,000.00**
Marketing	**3,500.00**	**1,000.00**	**1,000.00**	**5,500.00**

Total Other Costs	5,155.00	3,011.00	2,805.00	10,971.00
Total Expenses	67,665.00	61,463.00	57,056.00	186,185.00
EBIT (Operating Profit)	220,334.00	41,536.00	41,943.00	303,814.00

Team Budgets

Depending on your business, once you have staff they may require a budget to work towards. All my consultants in SpindaCorp had individual budgets. In the majority of cases these budgets will only need to include their own sales/revenue targets, unless the budget is for a manager, in which case you may also need to include expense and/or EBIT lines.

Have a look at the example below from SpindaCorp:

Staff Member	Service Line	January	February	March	Totals
James	GPs	$3,500.00	$3,500.00	$4,500.00	$11,500.00
	Specialists	$35,000.00	$0.00	$35,000.00	$70,000.00
	Juniors	$1,500.00	$1,500.00	$1,500.00	$4,500.00
	Totals for James	$40,000.00	$5,000.00	$41,000.00	$86,000.00

A well thought out and realistically set budget will create a strong sense of ownership from the team and will go a long way to boosting morale. Remember, these figures will act as the goal for your staff whose incentives are linked to achieving the budget. Having said this, if poorly put together, budgets can kill morale, piss your staff off and blow out your expenses.

It is my opinion that all businesses should have a budget and that ideally once set they should be fixed for the full FY. Usually completed about a month before the start of the next FY, I tend to review my budgets quarterly, but make no actual changes throughout unless something drastic has occurred either in the marketplace or within my business.

Setting budgets can be a time consuming and frustrating task if you want them done properly, taking anything from a couple of hours to a couple of days. All of my budgets within Goby were completely unrealistic and pointless as I kept changing them every couple of weeks. As a result I never had clear targets to work towards and it was almost like I would change them just to make myself feel better about how everything was going! Of course all this did was color reality and so it was no surprise looking back at it now that the business collapsed.

Lesson learnt, SpindaCorp was run a lot tighter, with budgets that were realistic, but slightly bullish. In your new business you can expect your first FY budget to be out of line with the real figures. Don't stress over this too much. As you get more experience running the business and thus a more intimate understanding of your market sector is developed, your ability to set achievable, but challenging targets will get better.

Calculating your budget

The Expense Component

The creation of your budget should always start with a look at your expenses for the coming year. Begin by tabling all of the expenses you anticipate and include items such as marketing costs, investment costs, purchase of new machinery, additional staffing costs, costs to source or manufacture products, etc.

Accuracy at this stage is vital if you want your overall budget to be correct and reflective of reality.

Remember this golden rule whenever creating any budget or forecast:

'If unsure about exact figures, always lean towards an overestimation of your expenses and an underestimation of your revenues' – a buffer is better than a big hole in your bank balance!

The Revenue Component

As mentioned before, you should always keep your budget realistic – bullish in a growing business, but not so bullish that it becomes unachievable and the joke of your team. This is especially important when you are setting individual or team budgets. Looking at my time working in sales roles, there is nothing more demoralizing to a team than having a budget set out that is not achieved month on month, yet the expectation is there that it has to be.

As a gesture to my team that their contribution is vital to the success of the company and to ensure I put an accurate budget together, I usually set budgets in consultation with individual members, listening to their views and thoughts on what they see for the coming 12 months.

Putting the actual document together, I've tried a number of different ways to create budgets, including using good old guesstimation! To be precise however you need to look at your business and answer the following question: do you get paid from clients by the hour or per product/service line? The answer to this will determine which of the below techniques will suit your business better.

Hourly Rate Scenario

For everyone in your business who completes work that is chargeable to a client (including yourself), use this

formula for each month of the year:

((hours per day x work days in month) – (hours per day x (annual leave days + sick days))) x hourly rate

= Estimated Max Revenue per month for that staff member

This formula is easy to set up in a spreadsheet, making it quite simple to use and time effective.

Important Note: What the formula assumes in this format is that the individual will be 100% productive at all times. Realistically though I can tell you that it will be rare for anyone to always be working at full capacity, so my recommendation would be to build in a factor that you think is reasonable to take this into consideration. As an example, if the workday has 7.5hrs available for billable work (after lunch breaks), perhaps you should factor in some time for non billable activities for things such as filing paperwork, checking emails etc. For example, 7.5hrs could become 6 hours. Also, by calculating on a month by month basis you can factor in potential dips due to things such as holiday periods. As an example, in SpindaCorp I found that the week before Christmas and the two weeks post New Years tended to be slow in the recruitment game, so I knew that billing even 6 hours of work per day during these periods was simply unrealistic.

If you want to add this into your spreadsheet modify the formula as such:

(((hours per day x work days in month) – (hours per day x (annual leave days + sick days)) x hourly rate) x actual hours / 100% hours

= Estimated Max Revenue per month for that staff member

Do the above for each month and you should get a pretty good estimate of expected work hours per employee. Now, you can either keep this as your budget or you can push the expectation higher by reducing the annual leave component and taking out the sick leave. This is especially recommended if you are creating budgets for any staff that will earn a bonus upon exceeding their budgets.

Remember though:

1. If creating budgets for staff, make them realistically challenging, but not so difficult that it becomes impossible to achieve.

2. Once set, only touch it if things drastically change either within your business or within your industry.

Per Product/Service

Creating a budget for businesses that generate revenue per product/service is a little bit trickier, especially for new businesses. If this is your first year in business then the best place to start is with your expenses. Work out how much you anticipate to spend running the business over 12 months, making sure you include a realistic income component for yourself. This total amount will now be the figure you have to achieve as a minimum for the financial year in order to break even, and can thus be used as the figure for your first budget.

Post first year, setting budgets will be done by analyzing your history of sales for prior years, looking at your expense plan for the current FY, looking at your growth goals and thus extrapolating your figures to become a budget.

The above method should suffice for the majority of businesses selling products to customers. If however your business sells products that you will be manufacturing in-house (e.g. hamburgers), then you will need to ensure that your available resources and pricing structure match up with the volumes you need to sell in order to cover your expenses and turn a profit.

If on the other hand you sell products and also provide services by the hour (e.g. a plumber who charges by the hour for services also sells you tap ware, showerheads etc.), then your budget should be a combination of the hourly rate scenario and the per product line scenario.

Cashflow Forecast Sheets

Forecast sheets track the financial result you think you will achieve over a given period of time. The main purpose of forecasting is to assist you in managing your cashflow, i.e. money coming in and money going out. By taking into account the amount of revenue you think you will generate during the week, you can ensure that your expenses are kept in check, with the aim of avoiding overspending.

I usually forecast three months in advance, using a cashflow forecast sheet similar to the one below (note that this is an example for one month only):

Revenue Forecast						
Cash in bank at start of month	$12,000.00					
Month: July	Week 1	Week 2	Week 3	Week 4	Week 5	Total
Product Line 1	$6,000.00	$3,500.00	$4,500.00	$4,000.00	$500.00	$18,500.00
Product Line 2	$4,000.00	$4,500.00	$5,100.00	$6,000.00	$1,200.00	$20,800.00

Service Line 1	$2,200.00	$3,000.00	$5,000.00	$4,000.00	$3,200.00	$17,400.00
Total Revenue	*$12,200.00*	*$11,000.00*	*$14,600.00*	*$14,000.00*	*$4,900.00*	*$56,700.00*

Expenses Forecast

Month: July	Week 1	Week 2	Week 3	Week 4	Week 5	Total
Staff	$7,500.00	$6,000.00	$6,500.00	$7,500.00	$1,500.00	**$29,000.00**
Premises	$0.00	$0.00	$0.00	$1,200.00	$0.00	**$1,200.00**
Communication	$0.00	$300.00	$0.00	$0.00	$0.00	**$300.00**
Travel	$0.00	$0.00	$0.00	$0.00	$0.00	**$0.00**
Entertainment	$120.00	$120.00	$120.00	$120.00	$0.00	**$480.00**
Motor Vehicle	$2,000.00	$150.00	$150.00	$150.00	$150.00	**$2,600.00**
Equipment	$0.00	$0.00	$0.00	$0.00	$0.00	**$0.00**
Financial	$0.00	$25.00	$0.00	$0.00	$0.00	**$25.00**
Admin	$0.00	$0.00	$90.00	$0.00	$20.00	**$110.00**
IT	$350.00	$0.00	$0.00	$0.00	$0.00	**$350.00**

Marketing	$4,300.00	$6,000.00	$5,000.00	$5,000.00	$600.00	**$20,900.00**
Total Expenses	*$14,270.00*	*$12,595.00*	*$11,860.00*	*$13,970.00*	*$2,270.00*	*$54,965.00*
Cashflow	Week 1	Week 2	Week 3	Week 4	Week 5	Cash End of Month
(cash in bank + revenue) - expenses	$9,930.00	$8,335.00	$11,075.00	$11,105.00	$13,735.00	**$13,735.00**

Forecasting is also a useful tool when you are looking at making large or out of the norm purchases for your business, or looking to re-invest your money into the business (for example putting on extra staff). By factoring this large expense into your forecast you can 'predict' to some degree (depending on how accurate your forecasts are) the impact this would have on your future cashflow, thereby enabling you to make an educated call whether this expense should occur, and whether it should occur at that particular point in time.

To equip yourself adequately in order to be able to make good forecast judgments, it is important you stay informed of what is happening within your industry, the economy and society in general. Knowing and understanding these factors will allow you to potentially see future problems and take action before the problems affect your business. While forecasting can be a great tool if used properly, I can tell you from firsthand experience that using incorrect information in your forecast sheets can make you blind to the real issues and can potentially make the realities look a lot more positive than they really are.

Remember how I told you in previous chapters about growing SpindaCorp pretty aggressively? There was a decision to put on staff based on the large amount of work that the business had coming in at an early stage. Well, much of the reasoning for doing this at the time came from my interpretation of the cashflow forecasting sheet that I had projected out over 12 months. Here is what I mean:

1. Although I was aware of the financial crisis that the world was facing and was aware of the tightening registration process for doctors, I did not account for this when drafting my cashflow forecast.

2. As a result of point #1, I did not build in any buffers in case of losing contracts and assumed a 100% success rate for contract completion.

3. To top this off, I made the mistake of accruing revenue from the date I received a signed contract, rather than accruing only such revenue when it had hit my bank account.

4. Although I built in a buffer of 3 months for a new starter to get up to speed and bring in money, this was not long enough and was well off the real timeframes.

As a result, the data that my cashflow forecast sheet initially contained was incorrect, and therefore led me to incorrectly make decisions based on this false data.

Earlier on I mentioned the need for business owners to sometimes don the 'devil's advocate hat' when making business decisions. The same thing applies when you are creating cashflow forecasts – think of the what if's and possible negative scenarios and build a buffer around this just in case things actually do turn sour.

Unfortunately for me, by the time I realized the implications of the financial crisis and tightening red tape on my business, I had overcapitalized on staff, eating into nonexistent revenue and thus digging a debt hole in the form of a heavily used overdraft facility.

Profit and Loss Statements (P&Ls)

P&Ls are usually generated out of the data contained within financial software. They are the actual results for a given period of time and are handy reports against which you can compare your budget and forecast figures. The layout of the P&L is similar to that of your budget – in fact many business owners use the P&L as the template for their budget and cashflow forecast sheets. There are numerous benefits to preparing P&Ls. Some of these include:

- Comparing forecasted and budgeted revenue with real, actual data.

- Compare past performance of your business with current performance.

- Assists you (or your bookkeeper/accountant) in preparing your annual tax returns.

Cashflow Management

Getting deep into debt with SpindaCorp all happened quickly – even regularly using budgets, P&Ls and cashflow forecasting, I miscalculated and made faulty decisions that were in the end irreversible. I realized the serious mistake we had made of spending money that hadn't yet been paid to the business only months after going down that path. Corrective action was taken by changing the forecasting and varying expenses to bring it in line with where it should have been months prior, but the problem was so ingrained that although it would have been possible to claw out of the hole, I needed more time and money than I had.

I will never forget the lesson that this taught me: **Building a business based on future revenue is like building a house out of cardboard – all is good while the sun shines, however rain only brings disaster.**

Cashflow management is more than just playing with spreadsheets. It is about correctly interpreting your financial data and using this knowledge to help direct the course your business travels.

At the heart of cashflow management is one simple truth: **cash is king!** With cash in the bank you have freedom and flexibility to do as you please, on your terms. To get to the level where your business is in a regularly strong positive cash situation will often take time, determination, mistakes and strategic planning.

I have seen many business owners, including myself, go through a phase with their business when things are booming and money is coming in the door. As I have experienced firsthand, the spending decisions business owners make during these boom times can mean the difference between surviving future downturns or sinking completely. During good times you may have the money to buy new toys and spend frivolously without counting your dollars, but do this without a buffer in place and your business will become that house built of cardboard. And the spending doesn't even have to be on toys or luxuries. It could be on too much stock, expensive over the top marketing campaigns or even an over commitment on staffing, similar to what occurred in SpindaCorp.

Unfortunately the world is an unpredictable place. As a result when you are running a business you can never rest completely at peace for the next day may bring a challenge that will test the foundations of your business. One way to ensure you get a good night's sleep however is to build a cash reserve in your bank account with which you can buy some time should your circumstances change. Use the above mentioned tools to monitor and track your financials. Be smart with your expenses, don't spend money for the sake of it, and make it your business to build enough cash reserves to keep all of your business expenses covered for at least 3 months without any income coming in. Now I know that this is going to be a big task to achieve; it can be hard enough to save $1,000 let alone many multiples of this. But it is achievable with budgeting, forecasting and smart cashflow management.

When you do have this cash, be smart and strategic with the additional profit. It will be at this point in time that a good accountant comes handy – don't forget that for every dollar in profit the tax man will want to take his share. Your accountant should be able to give you advice on the ways you can minimize your tax in line with the growth plans you have for your business. They will also be able to advise you on the smartest way to make large purchases for your business; items such as motor vehicles or shop fixtures, etc.

Going back to your revenue, the smartest thing (in my view – others will feel differently) you can do is to keep reinvesting the profit into your business to further strengthen your market share, increase your brand awareness and increase your profitability with the eventual goal that you can earn a passive income for the rest of your life, or to build up the value of your business enabling you to sell it for a very nice return.

Warren Buffett, one of the richest men on the planet, built up his empire in a similar manner. Warren initially started by setting up a couple of small businesses. He then invested all of his returns in the stock market, and as the investment grew, he kept re-investing all of the profits back into the purchase of more shares. After doing this for a number of years he had enough capital to start buying entire businesses. As he did so, he continued his reinvesting strategy of putting all profits back into his businesses. Throughout this period he lived below his means. Even when he reached the stage of multimillionaire status he didn't act like a millionaire, he never spent for the sake of it, and nor did he ever pursue materialistic obsessions. He would draw a salary enough to cover a comfortable life. Whilst this sort of lifestyle isn't for everybody (after all some of us want to enjoy other things in life apart from accumulating cash and assets), it has an important message – **if you want to become truly wealthy and build businesses for the long term then you must learn the art of cash management!**

I believe that it is important to avoid the traps of our materialistic 'I want it now' attitude culture. While times are great it may be very tempting to go buy yourself a new car or other such luxuries, perhaps even taking on personal loans from the business for holidays, but, this is a trap that can even end in bankruptcy as a worst case scenario. Just look back a few years to see the effects the US market crash had on high flying business men and women. Many were in control of highly profitable ventures, but as many were living in their extravagant homes and cars that had mortgages only payable with high incomes, when business crashed, so too did their personal lives. Homes were repossessed, cars were repossessed, and many went bankrupt. The same went not just for business owners but countless high flying executives, managers and others who were living a life not based on what they really needed, but based on how much they were earning. The truly wealthy people didn't get that way by spending as they could. And neither should you if you want to survive through business troughs.

Lessons on Sourcing More Money

Money is one of the most important subjects of your entire life. Some of life's greatest enjoyments and most of life's greatest disappointments stem from your decisions about money. Whether you experience great peace of mind or constant anxiety will depend on getting your finances under control. - Robert G. Allen

I need more money: Obtaining more Cash

As you read in my story I have experienced financial difficulties on a number of occasions, leading me to seek additional funding from various sources. If you find yourself as I did, running either out of cash, needing a top up whilst waiting for clients to pay you or needing more money to invest in the business, don't stress, you are not alone and it's not the end of the world! While money problems are incredibly stressful, there are several avenues for you to consider should you need more money. Before you make any decisions though or start talking to funders, go and have a very open and honest discussion with your accountant. I really wish I did this for both my businesses; it would have saved me a lot of money and a lot of headaches.

Walking into a meeting with your accountant the following questions should be asked:

1. Do you really need the extra money?
2. Can you re-jig your current expenses in such a way that you bypass or prolong the need to obtain additional funds?
3. If you do need money, what is the amount you need?
4. What is the easiest and cheapest way of acquiring additional funds?
5. How much will borrowed money really cost you (taking into account lending costs such as interest rate, monthly fees etc.)?
6. How will the repayment of the funds be managed?
7. What will the consequence be on your business if:
   a. You don't obtain extra funds?
   b. You obtain extra funds that are temporarily enough but prove insufficient and you need more funds at a later date?
   c. You can obtain extra funds but it is not as much as you need?

Used wisely, borrowed money can have fantastic benefits, but as many business owners will tell you, it is very very easy to trip over and fall into a never ending debt trap. My experience with debt and borrowed money is quite extensive, having relied on investors, credit cards, personal loans, over draft facilities and extended mortgages throughout the years. Getting your accountant involved when you need to make decisions about obtaining extra funds is critical, and with the answers to the above questions you will be better positioned to make a decision that will hopefully be the right one for you and your business.

Questions 1 and 7 are especially important. Often we get so carried away with our business that the big picture is not clearly seen. We may feel trapped financially or may think that without the funds to buy that new machine the business will not function. Question 1 is simple, but very powerful. You may not see another way, but as I have experienced firsthand, an outsider will see things from a different perspective and may well show you that you actually have no need at this stage for further funding. For example in Goby I obtained several thousand dollars from an investor to spend on business tools that I had thought were necessary. Looking back now, I see just how silly it was to purchase most of these items outright. In fact the business could have done without the extra funds. All I should have done was re-jig my expenses, cut back on certain non essential items and instead of spending thousands on a couple of larger items, I could have simply leased them for 6 months with the option to buy, extend or hand back at the end of the term. Had I gotten advice from my accountant I would have saved this money and the interest that it came with! A simple advice, but so easily missed.

Question 7 is a tough question to face up to. It may be easier to avoid such questions and just hope that you obtain the necessary funds, not worrying about any future needs. Hoping however won't take you far in business. It is thus imperative that you have answers to this question and are prepared for a worst case situation. What will really happen if you can't obtain extra funds? Can you still operate your business? And if you can get funds but it's not enough, is it worth taking on the debt and continuing with your business?

I faced this last question with Goby, but to my detriment I couldn't face the truth: although the idea was viable, it needed far more money invested into it to make it work than I could obtain.

I hid from this truth and only after getting further into debt and spending many hours stressing and worrying did I admit defeat. In the end I used up all of my available sources of funding and almost went bankrupt:

-   Personal loan
-   Credit cards maxed

- Parents
- Investors

So what are some of your options when it comes to sourcing funds?

Options for Sourcing Funds

Let's have a look at these to give you some ideas to discuss when you visit your accountant:

- Extended Credit Periods

- Credit Cards

- Overdraft Facility

- Cashflow Financing

- Business Loans

- External Investors

Extend Credit Periods with Suppliers

One of the most effective means of extending your available cash without actually borrowing more money is by asking for an extended payment period with your suppliers. Although most applicable to non-service businesses like a shop, this may even apply to you if you run a service business like SpindaCorp. In my

SpindaCorp example, I spent thousands of dollars every month on advertising with one particular job board, so to use my money more effectively I had the usual 30 day payment terms extended to 90 days, aligning this payment cycle closer to that of my debtors.

In most cases, in order for a supplier to be willing to do this for you and give your business extended credit, you must have done the following in the months and years prior:

1. Always paid on time or advised them if payment may be late, but always paid invoices without being hassled or chased for payment.

2. Built a positive relationship with the contact personnel.

3. Always kept suppliers in the loop with important changes or happenings within your business.

By doing all 3 over a period of about 18 months, I had no problems obtaining extra time to pay my advertising bills. In fact, they were very supportive of SpindaCorp and were appreciative that we were honest about the difficulties that we were going through. Interestingly I was never this open with my Goby suppliers and when I approached them for an extended payment period some even cancelled my line of credit and asked for money up front! In reality I didn't mean much to them as I didn't have a strong relationship that I could leverage.

The lesson in this is simple: **Always treat your suppliers like you would your customers. They may be your ace card in times of financial hardship.**

The danger with extended payment terms is in its misleading nature. All you are really doing by extending payment terms is delaying the moment when the bill is due and needs to be paid. By asking for extended terms the assumption will be there that come the due date you will have succeeded in building up enough reserves to pay off this debt in full. Of course we can't see into the future, and down the track you may well be in an even bigger pickle than the present position. As with all forms of debt, think twice before you go and take on more than you can chew!

Credit Cards

Whether it be for business or personal purchases, the first point of call for many people seeking extra money is credit cards. Used wisely, credit cards can be a great way of leveraging your cash and even obtaining free things. As you would with all major purchases, do your homework and shop around for the credit card that best suits your requirements.

The ease with which credit cards can be obtained can make them a serious trap for those short of funds – and if you think that there is a need for more than one card then perhaps you may want to seriously reconsider your options. **Beware holding multiple maxed out credit cards.**

Over the years I've had many credit cards, some proving very effective, others incredibly costly. Either in the haste to obtain funds or just simple naivety, often I didn't bother to read the fine print when applying for the cards and have been stung by things such as:

- High annual fees plus recurring fees for points programs.
- Ridiculously high interest rates following the expiration of a low introductory rate that eroded any benefits I would have gained from the honeymoon rate.
- Very high transaction fees and poor conversion rates for overseas purchases.
- Due to the high interest rates, paying the minimum amount per month consisted almost entirely of interest repayments, meaning that my principal amount hardly changed.

Credit cards however aren't all bad news. A close friend runs a business where he has to purchase tens of thousands of dollars worth of stock each month. He uses a very smart strategy to manage his expenses:

1. He uses the supplier credit period to the last day, paying bills the day before they are due, but never late (day 29 of a 30 day credit period).

2. He pays these bills with a credit card that offers a 52 day interest free period plus has a frequent fliers points program.

3. He pays off his card in full on day 51, starting the cycle again.

By doing this he not only has the full use of his own cash for 82 days (e.g. can leave it in a high interest bank account), but he also collects tens of thousands of frequent flier points each month. Every year he has enough points to travel anywhere in the world for free, simply through the smart use of his credit card. This is not the right option for everyone though, so involve your accountant and make a sensible decision.

Overdraft Facility

As opposed to credit cards where withdrawing cash is very expensive, overdraft facilities can be a good way of managing expenses while waiting for your clients to pay up. I used this facility with SpindaCorp on a regular basis, and found it particularly useful to help cover the cost of bills while I was waiting for my clients to pay invoices.

The problems I found with overdraft facilities:

1. To obtain one, the lender will in most cases require you to provide a security (such as your family house) over the loan. If the business runs into trouble and you can't make your repayments, your security can be seized.

2. Once approved it is very easy to access the money, which can cause problems if you are not a strong money manager. It can be very tempting to use the money for items that the money is not intended for (e.g. personal purchases).

3. Beware – if you step out of line with the overdraft terms the bank can step in and recall the overdraft amount, forcing you to pay up!

4. Overdrafts are great for managing cashflow ebbs, however are not effective if you want to purchase assets.

Overall I found the overdraft facility very easy to use and more cost effective than a credit card. The interest rate was better than most cards, although there are no interest free periods or frequent flyer points.

So how does it all work? Once your application is approved you will be notified by your bank that your overdraft is ready for use, usually set up under a checking account. As soon as you start using the facility you will start incurring interest on any amounts you have used. As you pay back any money you have withdrawn your facility is topped up and ready to be drawn down again.

Once set up, your overdraft facility will be available for the life of your business (unless you or the bank closes the account), making it a good backup to your daily operations.

A large proportion of businesses, from the small to the multinationals, use overdraft facilities as an effective cash management tool. You too may find this facility to work well for your business, and as long as you stay on top of the repayments without missing any, you shouldn't have any hassles from your bank.

Cashflow Financing

Another commonly used facility, cashflow financing gives businesses access to cash tied up in unpaid invoices.

Let's say you've been working solidly for a couple of months to close some large deals. You succeed, but one client wants 60 day payment terms and another wants 90 days. You would normally have no problems with this, but as you are running low on cash you were really banking on this money to land in your account sooner. This is where cashflow financing comes in, giving you the option to use your invoices as security to obtain an advanced payment on them from a credit facility.

Usually 70-90% of the value of the invoice will be accessible, and of course there will be a fee involved to do this. Once payment is received from your client, you pay the credit provider whatever is owed to them. This way you can run a business effectively without being stuck waiting through a 90 day payment period.

I used such a facility a couple of times within Goby, but due to the nature of the SpindaCorp business such a facility was not feasible. If you are confident that your invoice will be paid it could be a good option, but I would be wary of taking on debt over a dubious invoice as you could end up with a lot more headaches than you had bargained for if the invoice is not paid by your client.

Business Loans

Usually reserved for larger purchases such as vehicles, equipment and properties, loans can be an effective way of investing in your business now, without having to tie up large amounts of your cash. My personal experience with business loans was to use this facility to lease a motor vehicle for work purposes. With the interest fully tax deductible, it allowed me to immediately access a vehicle and not use my own cash upfront for it. What I found as a big drawback was the high interest rate and the inflexibility of the loan terms (e.g. penalties for early payment of the loan or caps on how much you can repay on the loan in a 12 month period).

External Investors

I've left the trickiest, most complicated of them all for last. Bringing on an external investor is a big decision; one which should be taken very seriously with the involvement of your accountant and solicitor. Your first challenge will be to actually source investors who would be interested in putting their hard earned cash into your venture.

Family and Friends

The first point of call for many business owners seeking investors is to turn to family, friends or other close contacts. In my case I had my parents and a family friend invest in Goby. I didn't have an agreement drawn up with my parents; I did have a very basic agreement with the family friend, but in reality I should have taken this agreement more seriously, with exact terms and conditions specified and drawn up by a solicitor.

How you do business with your friends and family is up to you and obviously depends on the relationship you have with them. For me, not having a formal arrangement with my parents worked well. The agreement on the other hand with the family friend was too simplistic and did not cover off well enough on important aspects such as the timeframe to repay the debt etc. This created some confusion in the end around the exact amount owed, and how the money was going to be paid back – a dilemma that a properly drawn up loan agreement would have avoided.

Angel investors/Venture Capital Firms

Professional investors are usually the option when large amounts of money are sought after. Sourcing such investors can be tricky – a good starting point is to search the web. To clarify these terms:

- **Angel investors:** Either individual investors or a group of investors who are seeking one or more opportunities to invest in.
- **Venture capital firms:** Professional organizations with the sole purpose of investing large amounts of money.

When it comes to professional investors you will have to dedicate enough time to prepare a business plan that will make your business the one that draws in their interest. It's important that you keep in mind that these investors would see a large number of business plans each year, investing in only a small fraction of these. As such, your plan needs to look, read and feel professional, with no mistakes, properly formatted, printed on good quality paper and neatly bound together. Nowadays submission would be accepted via email, but in my opinion nothing beats sending in a beautifully presented hardcopy.

Printing, formatting and binding is the easy bit. The content on the pages will be what truly determines whether your business is worthy of further investigation.

Unlike the relatively simple planning that I recommended when you started up your business, the business plan written up for external investors will have to be a very comprehensive document involving input from your accountant and potentially your solicitor. Going into the specifics of such a plan is outside my expertise; but I would recommend starting off by researching various business plan formats on the web, followed by meetings with your advisors. Once complete and submitted, it will often take a few weeks, or even months to receive any feedback. If your business meets the investors 'criteria' based on the submitted business plan, they will most likely want to meet you and may ask you to present the idea/business to their group.

Each organization will have their own due diligence procedure to follow, and this will probably involve their accountants and solicitors spending time with you and analyzing the proposal at hand. All going well, you can expect to receive an offer a number of months after initially submitting your business plan.

Unlike your family and friends who are often just happy to help you out and see some return on their investment, professional investors will be very demanding of you. Be prepared for tough negotiations. If in the end you can't come to an agreement favorable to both parties then you may be better off walking away, rather than locking yourself in a tight unfavorable contract.

Variety of Options

So as you can see, a variety of options exist that may be suitable for you to consider when seeking extra funds. It is important though that from the start of your business you are smart with your money, hopefully only turning to debt as a form of positive leverage to get ahead faster, as opposed to using debt as the only means of survival for your business.

Lessons on Winding Down your Business

How to fail in business

In the beginning of the book I said to you that business is harsh, that the majority of new ventures fail within the first couple of years.

Having gone through several ventures over the last 16 years (and counting), I have experienced firsthand the ups and downs that come with running businesses, and as a result I have become cautious and calculating with my moves. I don't intend to fail in existing and future ventures, but, knowing the realities, there will always be a chance that the cards come tumbling down. It is for this reason that I don't shy away from the topic of failure, and in fact I turn to it so that I can recognize the early warning signs that may just turn a negative into a success.

Sometimes, try as we might though, things get missed, mistakes are made and our plans for success are derailed. This chapter examines this in more detail and looks at how to fail correctly in your business.

I know it sounds odd, but yes, there is actually a strategy to fail correctly in business; it is a strategy that aims to minimize your losses and take you as far away from bankruptcy as possible. Before we look at this worst case scenario however, let's go back a bit and look at the lead up to the decision to wind down a business.

As I've mentioned several times throughout this book, being aware of the health of your business along with the market forces that affect your business is critical to enable you to spot trouble before it gets out of hand.

I put Goby into voluntary liquidation after months of financial problems, a costly move that could have been avoided had I understood my business a lot better. There were several warning signs that I either ignored or hoped would not cause me problems. The biggest of these came in the form of customer complaints and cancelled orders. Rather than tending to customer complaints and listening to what the market was telling me, I continued to push all of my products. In hindsight I should have really focused on the issues and understood where they were coming from, why they occurred and found a solution to them. It would have been sensible to take a few steps back when the whole logistics nightmare occurred and really focused on my core markets, building back my credibility and increasing the momentum gradually. By not being aware of just how tarnished Goby's reputation became, not listening to customers and not realizing just how important the marketing campaign was to the resulting sales, I stepped directly into the path of inevitable failure. The failure did come, and as I was unprepared I was forced into a scenario that did nothing to minimize my losses and took me just short of bankruptcy.

SpindaCorp was a different story. This time I was acutely aware of the health of my business and had in place several strategies to walk away from the business well before I actually did. Again, there were several warning signs that things were heading south, including:

1. Constant changes in red tape procedures and bureaucratic requirements that were hitting SpindaCorp hard, impacting revenue directly.

2. Financial issues:
    a. Stuart and I resorted to partial pay cuts, then stopped paying ourselves, then had to cut staff wages, finally letting go of staff or keeping them on commission only.
    b. Having to arrange partial payment of debt with suppliers and the Tax Office.

   c. Cutting back on spending and running at a bare minimum.

   d. Running the overdraft facility to almost zero.

 3. More and more arguments occurred with Stuart, especially over money.

Being very aware of the possibility that the business might fold, we looked at the best way to exit the business without burning either too much more money or having to make hasty unplanned decisions similar to the situation I found myself in with Goby. We came up with two strategies: primary and backup, incase primary failed.

The primary strategy involved multiple parts, completed simultaneously:

 1. Shift the focus of the business in line with the changing market environment, moving from Permanent recruitment to Locum contracting. Doing this would have allowed us to generate revenue at a much quicker pace, with the premise that this revenue could offset our mound of debt.

2. Advise everyone to whom we owed money of the situation the business was facing, and negotiate payment terms on this debt.

3. Cut costs as much as possible and shift staff out of the business.

4. Try and find a buyer for the business who can inject much needed capital and resources.

In theory it should have been easy to shift the focus away from the slow and difficult permanent medical recruitment to the fast paced locum contracting environment (which had much less red tape than the former style). Putting this into practice however was a different story. Never having done locum contracting before, I was stabbing in the dark, guesstimating what needed to be done. After months of trying it became very apparent that if we were to succeed at this then the whole business model had to change. Everything from the way we sourced doctors to the way we negotiated contracts and found clients was different. It was like setting up a new business all over again.

Had we decided to attempt the locum sector perhaps 12-18 months earlier, I am confident we would have pulled it off. As it was, we were running out of cash and simply did not have enough funds or time to make a decent push into the sector.

Tackling the financial problems was another matter.

A critical part of any exit strategy should look at how you are going to tackle the financial problems you are having. In the vast majority of cases, money will be owed to third parties, a reality that you must not hide from if this is the case. The last thing you need at this stage are angry creditors threatening to take action against you if you don't pay up. So as part of your strategizing, involve your creditors. Go and either meet with them in person (preferred) or give them a call. Tell them your situation, advise them that you intend to do everything you can to pay off your debt, and then see if you can come to some sort of a compromise around this. Note: **Don't leave this to the last minute. Give your creditors ample notice, otherwise it will be thrown back at you.**

We contacted all of our creditors, met with them face to face where possible, and had lengthy discussions about our situation, our plans moving forward and then negotiated the repayment terms. Not one of the creditors was nasty to us, and all were happy to assist us with a repayment plan. Of course they knew that if we call bankruptcy chances are they would end up with nothing, so the more they helped us the higher the chances of them recouping their money.

This worked very well for us, and with all of the creditors from the banks to the Taxation office off our backs, we had more of a breathing space to think about our next steps, which included agreeing on our respective debt amounts and selling the business.

Although the company was facing problems, the actual business idea of recruiting doctors (especially locums) was still very profitable and viable. We had accumulated a huge database of doctors and had contacts in almost every hospital and major medical facility in Australia. What we needed was a serious injection of cash and some better resources in terms of staffing and office support. To achieve this we attempted to sell the business. Our goals were to find a company that could provide the above, keep Stuart and myself as directors/managers and keep our current staff, but give them a decent salary.

Sourcing interested parties was quite easy at first as a lot of recruitment agencies were looking at entering the medical sector. We held meetings with a number of potential suitors and some of these progressed to multiple meetings and serious offer discussions. Unfortunately for us as the global economic downturn rapidly worsened, our suitors started pulling out one by one, simply not willing to invest under such uncertain times. Those that remained drove a hard, inflexible bargain. We had one solid offer on the table, but it was so restrictive and inflexible that we were not willing to step into a potentially highly stressful uncompromising situation.

This is where the backup strategy kicked in. With the reinvigoration and proposed sale of the business failing, there was only one solution left: split up the debt and each of us takes on our respective share enabling us to walk away from the business. This debt issue however was a challenging one: just how do we split the debt up should the business close and who owes what amount to SpindaCorp?

This was a topic we argued over for weeks. It was at this point that I wished we documented more of the financial dealings amongst the two of us, rather than relying on the 'gentleman's handshake'. Refer back to the Lessons on Business Partners section for information on business partners and financial matters.

The final months went by very fast. The business ran out of cash and with that it ran out of momentum. I had already survived for months with no income and had come to my last reserves of personal savings. With all options exhausted and the debt split finally agreed to with Stuart, I stepped down as director and sought employment elsewhere.

Goby, as you know, was put under voluntary liquidation. In the end, SpindaCorp was simply shelved, with all debt being transferred out of the business and taken on personally by Stuart and myself. I avoided liquidating or bankruptcy, however, this was only an option as I was able to extend the mortgage on our house in order to take on my portion of the debt.

If you are faced with having to close your business like I did, what options do you have? The list below will give you some guidance on suitable exit options (bear in mind that the information below starts from the worst case scenario down):

Bankruptcy

This is the worst case scenario and the one you should avoid if at all possible. Going bankrupt will personally affect you for a lengthy time, with ramifications that can include the cancellation of your passport and inability to borrow money for things such as property (or if loans are accessible, then chances are you will be slugged with huge fees and interest rates). If you fully co-operate with the Trustee overseeing the bankruptcy then it will last for 3 years, although it can be extended to 5 or 8 years under certain circumstances (this was correct at time of writing, so please talk to your solicitor for exact accurate information at the time).

Important note: guarantors or joint borrowers (for example a business partner), will still be liable for the full debt even if you call bankruptcy, unless they themselves go bankrupt.

Most people think that bankruptcy clears you of all debt; this however is a big misnomer. If you go bankrupt in Australia and earn a salary from employment after calling bankruptcy, then you may (dependent on the amount of your income and personal circumstances) be forced to make repayments out of your salary towards this debt. The amount depends on a number of factors, but it means you can't just walk away from not having to pay up.

By going bankrupt, you need to keep in mind the following:

- As a bankrupt you will most likely lose all of your assets and will have to start life from scratch.

- As a bankrupt you will be restricted with undertaking certain types of employment, such as being a security guard or joining the police force. You will also be barred from becoming a director of another company without the prior permission from the court.

- As a bankrupt you will be restricted from holding a variety of licenses including builder's license, principal real estate agents license, liquor license, financial brokering license and more.

- Whilst bankrupt, if you purchase certain types of assets they may be seized and sold by the Trustee.

- Travel overseas will be heavily restricted, and you will need to jump through a number of hoops in order to get approval from the Court to do so.

As you can see it's not a pretty picture overall, hence why I do everything to avoid this like the plague!

Liquidation

Voluntary

If you reach a point when you can't manage your debt, you have no more cash, have some assets such as stock and have exhausted all your means of getting additional funds and can't trade your way out of the debt, then voluntarily calling in liquidators may be an option.

I put Goby through this process. The steps taken to undergo voluntary liquidation:

1. Decision to commence liquidation is started by the directors or shareholders of the company.

2. Liquidator appointed.

3. Liquidator investigates the affairs of the company, completes a very thorough assessment of your business and will take over dealing with the debt.

4. Liquidator draws up the list of creditors. A creditors report and notice of meeting are sent out. In most cases they will negotiate an arrangement with your creditors and suppliers that clears the debt.

5. Usually liquidation is completed within 12 months; however in some cases the process is more complex and can take several years.

In general, assets are paid out as follows:

1. Employees.

2. Secured creditors (e.g. banks).

3. Unsecured creditors.

One negative I found with liquidating was the cost involved; had I not been able to secure the money to cover the cost of the liquidator the situation could have forced me into bankruptcy. Still, it's worth the homework and the money. The actual process is tedious and labor intensive, but better than the alternative of bankruptcy. Interestingly I found the process to be a great learning tool. I asked tons of questions from my liquidators and gained an insight into the arrangements which creditors and suppliers could possibly be willing to take on to re-coup at least a small portion of their funds.

It was a lot of this knowledge that helped me understand just how important my relationship with creditors and suppliers is, and the importance of keeping them informed about the health of my business.

Involuntary

Usually instigated when a creditor (most commonly) applies to the court for the company to be wound up (liquidated) on the basis of insolvency. The applicant must prove to the court that they (the company in question) are in fact insolvent and cannot pay its debt when due. As part of the process the creditor can issue a demand on the company, requiring it to pay the debt within a specified time period. Should this not occur or should an alternative arrangement fail to be reached, the creditor may apply to the court for the winding up.

Non compliance with this order creates a presumption of insolvency which needs to be disproved by the company if it is to prevent the wind up proceeding. The process is complicated and legal advice will be required should this occur to you.

Take on the debt

This is the option I prefer as it leaves no trace from a credit rating point of view (if done correctly) and leaves your personal reputation intact. For me, it is also a moral and ethical way of ending a business. It is not just the big banks that get affected when a business runs into trouble – some of your suppliers may be small businesses as well, so not abiding by the promise to pay them could seriously affect those businesses as well.

This option however is only an option if you can plan your exit strategy in advance (as per my example with SpindaCorp), and if:

1. You can access additional funds for the purpose of paying out the debt (now or in the future). Or,
2. You can gain immediate employment elsewhere and afford to repay your debt as per the agreements you negotiated with your creditors.

With SpindaCorp I turned to both of the above options. Whilst working on the exit strategy about 6 months from actually walking away, I knew that the house I bought several months before would in the next 12-18 months have enough equity in it to pay out my portion of the debt. The problem was though that when I walked away from the business neither Stuart nor I could pay out our debt in the entirety. So, a repayment schedule was negotiated with all creditors and we each agreed to pay back a certain amount per month from our personal incomes to the business. I also stayed at SpindaCorp until I had a job lined up, giving me the confidence that I could afford to make the repayments. Although the payments were high and my wife and I really suffered financially as a result, I managed to keep on top of the payments until finally we had the equity available in the house to draw upon and pay out the debt, taking over it personally.

While this was waiting to occur the business was put into limbo, not trading, just sitting idle until the debt was transferred out.

To make a smart, logical decision around closing a business, you must involve your advisors. Take your feelings out of the process, stay levelheaded and keep your cool throughout. No doubt if you have to go through such an experience it will be very taxing on you both financially and emotionally. Rather than getting angry, frustrated or any of those other negative emotions, try and use this time to learn and reflect.

Needless to say I have taken a huge financial battering over the years, but with positive attitude and a lot more knowledge thanks to the mistakes made, I look forward to a more financially secure future!

Post Business Blues

Like most other countries, Japan was hit badly by the Great Depression of the 1930s. In 1938, Soichiro Honda was still in school when he started a little workshop, developing the concept of the piston ring.

His plan was to sell the idea to Toyota. He laboured night and day, even slept in the workshop, always believing he could perfect his design and produce a worthy product. He was married by now, and pawned his wife's jewellery for working capital.

Finally, came the day he completed his piston ring and was able to take a working sample to Toyota, only to be told that the rings did not meet their standards! Soichiro went back to school and suffered ridicule when the engineers laughed at his design.

He refused to give up. Rather than focus on his failure, he continued working towards his goal. Then, after two more years of struggle and redesign, he won a contract with Toyota.

By now, the Japanese government was gearing up for war. With the contract in hand, Soichiro Honda needed to build a factory to supply Toyota, but building materials were in short supply. Still he would not quit! He invented a new concrete-making process that enabled him to build the factory.

Realities of Business: Misadventures and Lessons Learnt

With the factory now built, he was ready for production, but the factory was bombed twice and steel became unavailable, too. Was this the end of the road for Honda? No!

He started collecting surplus gasoline cans discarded by US fighters – "Gifts from President Truman," he called them, which became the new raw materials for his rebuilt manufacturing process. Finally, an earthquake destroyed the factory.

After the war, an extreme gasoline shortage forced people to walk or use bicycles. Honda built a tiny engine and attached it to his bicycle. His neighbours wanted one, and although he tried, materials could not be found and he was unable to supply the demand.

Was he ready to give up now? No! Soichiro Honda wrote to 18,000 bicycles shop owners and, in an inspiring letter, asked them to help him revitalize Japan. 5,000 responded and advanced him what little money they could to build his tiny bicycle engines. Unfortunately, the first models were too bulky to work well, so he continued to develop and adapt, until finally, the small engine 'The Super Cub' became a reality and was a success. With success in Japan, Honda began exporting his bicycle engines to Europe and America.

End of story? No! In the 1970s there was another gas shortage, this time in America and automotive fashion turned to small cars. Honda was quick to pick up on the trend. Experts now in small engine design, the company started making tiny cars, smaller than anyone had seen before, and rode another wave of success.

Today, Honda Corporation employs over 100,000 people in the USA and Japan, and is one of the world's largest automobile companies. Honda succeeded because one man made a truly committed decision, acted upon it, and made adjustments on a continuous basis. Failure was simply not considered a possibility. Source: cited on the Honda Worldwide website and several other websites.

Depression and Beyond

Starting your own business, making it grow, investing all those hours and emotions and then to have it all collapse is just heartbreaking.

Ending Goby left me depressed. SpindaCorp was a bit easier on me emotionally in that I avoided depression, but I still took an emotional battering. To fail once is bad enough, but to fail for the second time did not sit well with me. For a while I played the blame game, telling myself that I am incompetent, belittling myself and really thinking very little of my skills and abilities. In truth, I was very embarrassed about the situation and my ego and confidence were shot.

Overcoming all those negative emotions was high on the list after SpindaCorp for I knew that, as I had after Goby, it would be very quick and easy to spiral into depression again.

What I experienced after the end of both my businesses is something I call the Post Business Blues (PBB). While I found it unavoidable to miss second time around, I did learn that it is possible to minimize the duration and severity of PBB.

Healthy mind and healthy body

Looking after your health and wellbeing is important if you want to enjoy life to its full. It is also important if you are to have the strength and resilience (both psychological and physical) to bounce back from highly stressful situations that may come your way whilst running your own business. This is especially important when the business you have spent so much time and energy on collapses. One of the reasons why I believe that I dealt so well with PBB after SpindaCorp was not only because I was better prepared second time around, but also because I was physically and emotionally much stronger and together than in the past. Knowing full well that the end of the business was nearing, my exit strategy also included an emotional health component.

While I couldn't escape getting down and feeling sorry for myself, I did prevent depression and I also shortened the period that the blues lasted. Getting past the PBB came down to three things.

The first component involved opening up to my family and friends. I especially turned to my wife for emotional support (thank you Kitty!) and my brother who, being a solicitor, always had some real world words of wisdom to snap me out of my blues. My parents were also involved. I talked to them a lot and they knew from previous experience the importance listening and support plays during times like these.

The second component involved a lot of internal thinking and reflection over SpindaCorp. I would spend my time in the car driving with no music or sound, just quiet, allowing me to think about the experience I went through. I would use as much of my alone time as possible to just think, look at all my mistakes and achievements and store them in my memory bank ready to turn to at a later stage. I learnt to not beat myself up over events in the past and the more I understood and reflected, the calmer my mind got.

The third and last component involved a lot of reading. When I got busier and busier in my businesses I put reading books on business, success and motivation to the side. I picked up on those books again post SpindaCorp, boosting my motivation and again making me realize that there is no point being beat, it's much more fun and exciting being happy, motivated and optimistic.

The Journey Forward

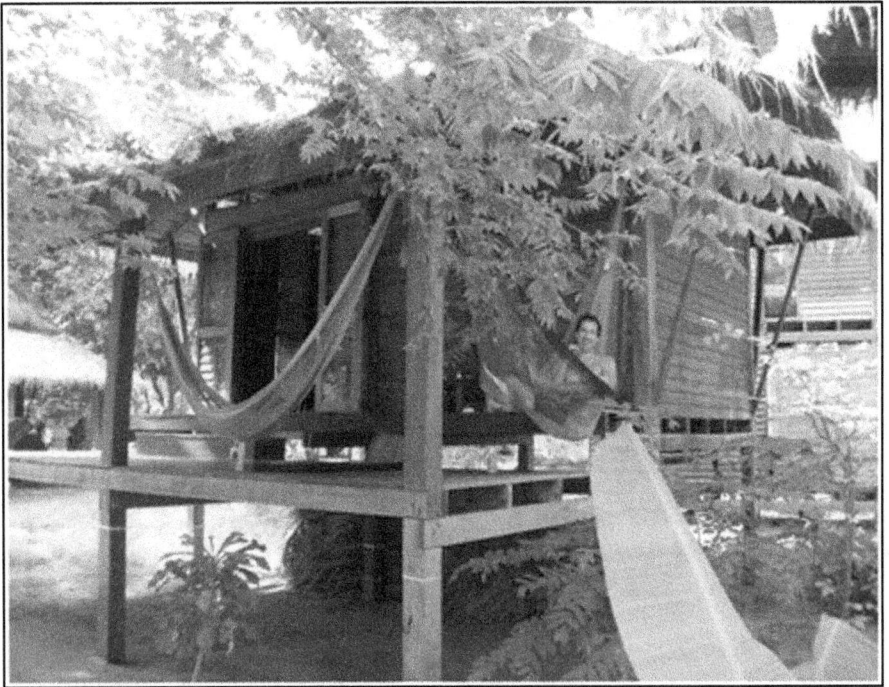

Above: Me lying in a hammock on the island of Koh Lipe, Thailand, writing this book.

Life is definitely a rollercoaster ride. There are ups and downs and unexpected twists and turns that shake your core beliefs and values. I strongly believe that one can always learn and grow from negative, difficult and challenging events that we face throughout our journeys. It took me a long time to embrace this fact, as I have not only gone through significant business stress over the years, but also personal events have occurred to me (and my wife) that at times left me questioning life itself.

I decided to write this book to not only help others achieve their business dreams, but to help me learn more about myself. During the 18 or so months it took to write the manuscript, my wife and I took 6 months out of normal life to travel and enjoy something I had never allowed myself before: time just for me and my partner, to do what we wanted without any commitments, stress or social influence. We travelled the world, ate all sorts of weird and wonderful food, experienced many different cultures and spent a lot of time doing absolutely nothing! While travelling around the world, much of this book was written - some chapters came to life whilst I was sitting in a hammock on the tiny island of Koh Lipe off the coast of Thailand. Other chapters took shape as I lay rugged up beside a warm heater, sipping hot tea in a beautiful little villa in the Alps of Northern Italy while snow gently fell outside.

Life is what you make it. Embrace your talents and aim for the stars!

It's important to point out that the advice I give you in this book is the same advice I give myself. I follow the lessons I outlined and having learnt from the mistake of growing too fast, my businesses are now very controlled in terms of how fast they are growing, ensuring that my growth keeps up with my capabilities, systems and processes. I have no debt in the businesses. I run cashflow positive at all times, and the future is looking incredibly promising.

And so my story continues, and hopefully the journey I take will inspire other entrepreneurs along the way.

In closing, if there is only one message you take out of this book, then it should be this one:

> *If you think you are beaten, you are. If you think you dare not, you don't! If you want to win, but think you can't, it's almost a cinch you won't. If you think you'll lose, you're lost. For out in the world we find success begins with a fellow's will. It's all in the state of the*

mind. Life's battles don't always go to the stronger and faster man, but sooner or later the man who wins is the man who thinks he can. – Walter D. Wintle

I really hope that sharing my experiences will help you achieve great success in business and life.

Cheers to your success!

Pete

Glossary of Terms

Accountant: A professional whose job it is to keep, audit, and inspect the financial records of individuals or businesses. They prepare financial and tax reports, and can also provide advice on a variety of finance related topics such as taxation. Source: Wikipedia.

Accrue: In economics and accounting, means to increase by growth or addition.

Bankruptcy: Is a legal status of an insolvent person or an organization, that is, one that cannot repay the debts owed to creditors. Source: Wikipedia.

Book Keeper: Is an individual whose job it is to keep financial records for an individual or business.

Calendar Year: The 12 month period starting from the 1st of January to the 31st of December of a given year.

Cashflow: The movement of money coming in and going out.

EBIT: Earnings Before Interest and Tax. This is the profit generated as a result of business activities, before any interest or taxation has been taken out.

Expense: Money spent on something.

Financial Year: The 12 month period starting from the 1st of July to the 30th of June (in Australia).

Insolvency: Inability to pay creditors the sums owed, or, put in other words, an individual who cannot pay their debts when they are due.

Liquidation: Sale of the assets of a business in order to cover its debts. This usually ends in the winding up of the business in question.

Liquidator: A person appointed to wind up the affairs of a business. Source: www.dictionary.com.

Net Profit: This is what you are after as a business owner. This term represents the actual profit your business has generated after all expenses including taxes etc., has been taken out of the revenue.

P&L: Profit and Loss statement. A document that outlines whether a business is making money or not over a period of time (and by how much), by factoring in the total actual revenue and expenses of that business.

Revenue: Amount of money coming into a business.

Spreadsheet: A computer program used predominantly for accounting, in which figures are arranged in the rows and columns of a grid. Source: Wikipedia.

Trust: Legal arrangement in which money or property is managed by one person (or organization) for the benefit of another. Source: Public Trustee SA.

Trustee: An individual or organization which holds or manages and invests assets for the benefit of another. Source: www.investorwords.com.

Visit my website for additional material, information on my seminars, news on upcoming books and much more!

www.peterspinda.com

And visit Digital Duet for everything web for business!

www.digitalduet.com.au

ISBN: 978-0-9872627-6-9

www.ingramcontent.com/pod-product-compliance
Lightning Source LLC
Chambersburg PA
CBHW060327200326
41519CB00011BA/1856